Verse *for the Day*

More than just another daily devotional!

Jane,
May God bless you with a Divine
awareness of His presence in
your life every day!
Y.B.I.C.
Linda
11/17/2016

Becoming more aware of God's presence in our daily lives
Feeding the soul

Inspired by the Holy Spirit
Written by: Lincoln S. Kokaram

outskirtspress
DENVER, COLORADO

Outskirts Press, Inc.
http://www.outskirtspress.com

ISBN: 978-1-4787-6882-1

Outskirts Press and the "OP" logo are trademarks belonging to Outskirts Press, Inc.

PRINTED IN THE UNITED STATES OF AMERICA

PREFACE

The Verse for the Day started approximately 14 years ago with one person and has grown organically to 190 followers. Many of the 190 forward the verse to their friends and family, so I have no idea of how many lives are impacted.

The Verse for the Day is directly inspired by the Holy Spirit. I never know what the verse will be until I pray and open the Bible. The commentary is also totally inspired by the Holy Spirit. I pray that your spiritual life will be impacted in a positive way and you will grow closer to Jesus every day.

GUIDE – HOW TO GET THE MOST
OUT OF THE VERSE FOR THE DAY

Read the verse and commentary first thing every morning. Complete the 3 statements before going to bed at night. This is intended to help us become more aware of the presence of the Lord in our personal life.

1. God blessed me today when He… *(Note a specific blessing that you alone received from God. It does not have to be a big thing. Please do not write that you woke up. Many non-believers woke up also.)*

2. God used me today when I … *(Note one thing that you did today to glorify our Lord. How did you obey His command?)*

3. I need to ask God to forgive me today for… *(Note one sin you committed today.)*

FOREWORD

The Verse for the Day acts as a reminder of who I am in Christ and encourages me to remain steadfast. More importantly though, it has helped me to strengthen my prayer life. I actually look forward to the prayer requests so I can pray for each situation.

Claudile Sydial
Ocho Rios, Jamaica

"I look forward every day to your "Verse of the Day". It is so great to take a short break at the beginning of my day and put all the hustle and bustle aside and read the verse and your devotion. It has become a vital part of my day and my spiritual walk. Thank you again for all the time and effort you put into this each day."

God Bless,
Tim
Atlanta, USA

This has been a very inspirational part of my life! I use this each day to get my priorities right! Often times your message is parallel to the message I receive at church each week and I know I need the repetition! "Practice makes permanent." Also, I have four children and I copy and text this to them each morning. It has helped me be more introspective and thankful for all the wonderful gifts from God: Our health, our beautiful world etc. It's also very encouraging to help others in need through prayer and know that so many others are praying on my behalf.

Steve
Springfield, KY

I look forward to them each day. They are very inspirational.

Roland
Atlanta, USA

These daily verses appear to be amazingly personalized to my life and show me that I am a child of Christ. The learnings are life lessons. They celebrate with me, comfort and guide me through difficult times and generally are encouraging and uplifting. You are the conduit between God and us. Thanks to you and MH for your commitment.

God bless,
Germaine
Trinidad & Tobago

One of the first things I do each day is to look for your email with the verse for that day. After reading the verse, I can always apply it to some part of my life. And in doing so, it gives me great satisfaction that when I slip and fall into the negative, God is always there to pick me up! For that, I am so grateful as the burden is not mine to handle. He has a plan designed specifically for me!!"

Mary
Philadelphia, PA, USA

Lincoln's Verse for the Day offers daily nuggets of truth that often seem to hit me at just the right time. The Bible is a collection of writings that together make up one pretty thick book, which at times can seem overwhelming. The Verse for the Day simplifies approaching the Bible by offering a single verse or small passage with a succinct and concise thought. This brevity and simplicity offers a great onramp for new Christians, a point of recalibration for biblical scholars, and encouragement for everyone in between.

Jonathan
Atlanta, USA

This has impacted my life by reminding me each day that we are all here on earth as brothers and sisters for a higher purpose. Each day when I read the verse, it reminds me that I am a daughter of God and there is a plan if I follow his words.

Janet
Utah, USA

Verse for the Day has blessed me by consistently glorifying God and being biblically sound. This ministry, delivered by a humble servant of God, brings together a disparate group of believers from all walks of life to worship our Lord daily. I've known Linc for over a decade both professionally and personally; he genuinely cares for the spiritual well being of each of us, the Verse of the Day recipients. He signs his correspondence; Y.B.I.C. and I truly feel that he is my 'brother in Christ'.

In His grip,
Jen
Atlanta, GA

JANUARY 1

May the peace of our Lord Jesus Christ be with you!

> *"and the enemy who sews them is the devil. The harvest is the*
> *end of the age, and the harvesters are angels."*
> *Matthew 13:39 NIV*

We are engaged in a constant spiritual battle. Some of us are aware of it while many don't give it a second thought. This attitude is dangerous and very risky. We need to know that the real enemy is the devil. He exists, and his mission is to separate us from the love and protection of Jesus Christ. Let us not become complacent. May we always be on the lookout for his attacks. May we always stand behind Jesus our protector and shield.

Have a Blessed Day! Follow Him! One Less Day to Go!

God blessed me today, when He:

_____
_____
_____

God used me today when I:

_____
_____
_____

I need to ask God to forgive me today for:

_____
_____
_____

JANUARY 2

May the peace of our Lord Jesus Christ be with you!

> *"He who dwells in the shelter of the Most High will rest in the shadow of the Almighty."*
> Psalm 91:1 NIV

As we enter another year, may we dwell in the shelter of our Lord and Savior. May we draw closer to Him and seek His direction every day. May He grant us the wisdom to know His will for us and the discipline to obey Him.

May this year be full of opportunity to serve our Father and introduce many to Him.

Have a Blessed Day! Follow Him! One Less Day to Go!

God blessed me today, when He:

_____

_____

_____

God used me today when I:

_____

_____

_____

I need to ask God to forgive me today for:

_____

_____

_____

_____

JANUARY 3

May the peace of our Lord Jesus Christ be with you!

> *"Cast all your anxiety on Him because He cares for you."*
> *1 Peter 5:7 NIV*

Every one of us experiences some level of anxiety at different times in our lives. Jesus wants us to cast our anxieties on Him. What a Father! We do not have to deal with our anxieties on our own. We have a God who says "Cast all your anxiety on Me." Why? Because He cares for us.

We do not have to earn this care or be good enough. It is so simple; He cares for you and me. Be aware that the devil will try his best to confuse us into believing that God would not care for us. But our God says it clearly. Therefore the next time you are faced with some anxiety cast it on Him and leave it there.

Have a Blessed Day! Follow Him! One Less Day to Go!

God blessed me today, when He:

_____

_____

_____

God used me today when I:

_____

_____

_____

I need to ask God to forgive me today for:

_____

_____

_____

_____

JANUARY 4

May the peace of our Lord Jesus Christ be with you!

> "But in your hearts set apart Christ as Lord. Always be pre-
> pared to give the reason for the hope that you have. But do
> this with gentleness and respect."
> 1 Peter 3:14 NIV

Many believers and non-believers have already broken their New Year's resolution. Here is some advice from St. Peter for all of us to consider this year. When people ask us what is our faith or what do we believe in; do we have a quick, simple, clear and confident response? Do our lives reflect the image of Jesus or contradict it? Do we stand out or fit in? Do we conform to the ways of this world? May God bless us with His power to shine as bright lights that show the way to Him and may many find Him this year because of our invitation. Share your faith with someone today - by word or action.

Have a Blessed Day! Follow Him! One Less Day to Go!

God blessed me today, when He:

_____
_____
_____

God used me today when I:

_____
_____
_____

I need to ask God to forgive me today for:

_____
_____
_____

JANUARY 5

May the peace of our Lord Jesus Christ be with you!

> *"God's voice thunders in marvelous ways; He does great things beyond our understanding."*
> *Job 37:5 NIV*

Our God is so great that we cannot understand or explain the many things He does. That's why our faith must be strong. If we could explain everything about God, then we would not need to have faith. We will be like Him. A day will come when we will be one with Him and be able to understand everything about Him. In the meantime may our faith be strong. He will manifest as we grow in faith.

Have a Blessed Day! Follow Him! One Less Day to Go!

God blessed me today, when He:

_____
_____
_____

God used me today when I:

_____
_____
_____

I need to ask God to forgive me today for:

_____
_____
_____

JANUARY 6

May the peace of our Lord Jesus Christ be with you!

> *"For we are to God the aroma of Christ among those who are being saved and those who are perishing."*
> *2 Corinthians 2:15 NIV*

Unbelievable, isn't it? That God describes us as "the aroma of Christ." That is, those who are being saved. Do you feel as if you are being saved or perishing? If you really believe that Jesus died on the cross for your sins and accept Him as Lord and Savior, then you are being saved and you my brother and sister are "the aroma of Christ" to God. Wow!

Have a Blessed Day! Follow Him! One Less Day to Go!

God blessed me today, when He:

_____
_____
_____

God used me today when I:

_____
_____
_____

I need to ask God to forgive me today for:

_____
_____
_____

JANUARY 7

May the peace of our Lord Jesus Christ be with you!

> *"Sustain me according to Your promise, and I will live; do not let my hopes be dashed."*
> *Psalm 119:116 NIV*

Do you know the promises of the Lord? He will never leave us nor forsake us. He has gone to prepare a place for us and He will come back for us. If we believe and confess our sins, He will forgive us. We will receive a new body. We will be one with Him. We will have trials and tribulations in this world. His grace is sufficient. He will not destroy the earth by flood. God keeps his promises. Our strength comes from Him. If we stay connected to His spirit, our hopes will not be dashed.

Have a Blessed Day! Follow Him! One Less Day to Go!

God blessed me today, when He:

_____
_____
_____

God used me today when I:

_____
_____
_____

I need to ask God to forgive me today for:

_____
_____
_____

_____

JANUARY 8

May the peace of our Lord Jesus Christ be with you!

> *"The silver is mine and the gold is mine declares the Lord Almighty."*
> *Haggai 2:8 NIV*

We must remember that all things come from the Lord. He owns everything. Anything we think we own is simply a gift from Him to use to glorify Him. The last funeral I went to I looked in the coffin and all I saw was the body, nothing else. May we learn to be good stewards of God's riches while we live on this earth.

Have a Blessed Day! Follow Him! One Less Day to Go!

God blessed me today, when He:

_____

_____

_____

God used me today when I:

_____

_____

_____

I need to ask God to forgive me today for:

_____

_____

_____

JANUARY 9

May the peace of our Lord Jesus Christ be with you!

"But who are you, O man, to talk back to God? Shall what is formed say to Him who formed it, "Why did You make me like this?" "
Romans 9:20 NIV

If we could learn to accept ourselves in the way God created us, we will have so much less frustration and anxiety in this world. Too many of us are trying to re-shape ourselves to look like someone else. We must remember that God only made one of each of us. We are all unique, yet in His image. How can we improve on God's creation? May we learn to be more content in what God has made and enjoy it while we are here. He has promised that we will all receive a new body. Meanwhile, let us make the best of the one we have.

Have a Blessed Day! Follow Him! One Less Day to Go!

God blessed me today, when He:

_____
_____
_____

God used me today when I:

_____
_____
_____

I need to ask God to forgive me today for:

_____
_____
_____
_____

JANUARY 10

May the peace of our Lord Jesus Christ be with you!

> *"You, dear children are from God and have overcome them,*
> *because the One who is in you is greater than the one who is*
> *in the world."*
> *1 John 4:4 NIV*

Life in this world is a continuous battle. The evil one is always on the attack. We who believe are like trophies for him. The only way we are able to overcome the temptations of this world and obey our Lord is because He is in us. It is by His grace and power we are able to overcome any evil. So may we always call on Him in the time of trials and temptations and be bold to say, like Jesus, "In the name of Jesus Christ, I command you - get thee behind me Satan."

Have a Blessed Day! Follow Him! One less Day to Go!

God blessed me today, when He:

_____

_____

_____

God used me today when I:

_____

_____

_____

I need to ask God to forgive me today for:

_____

_____

_____

JANUARY 11

May the peace of our Lord Jesus Christ be with you!

> *"As the rain and the snow come down from heaven, and do not return to it without watering the earth and making it bud and flourish, so that it yields seed for the sower and bread for the eater, so is My word that goes out from My mouth: It will not return to Me empty, but will accomplish what I desire and achieve the purpose for which I sent it."*
> *Isaiah 55:10 & 11 NIV*

Some may think that Jesus died for nothing, but God's word is clear, He will not return empty. Our Lord was and is victorious. He achieved what He came to do, to save us from our sins and to open a way for us to go to heaven. Now we choose. Will we be one of His chosen or will we choose to follow the evil one? Let us feed on the Word and live God's purpose.

Have a Blessed Day! Follow Him! One Less Day to Go!

God blessed me today, when He:

_____

_____

_____

God used me today when I:

_____

_____

_____

I need to ask God to forgive me today for:

_____

_____

_____

JANUARY 12

May the peace of our Lord Jesus Christ be with you!

> *"For the upright will live in the land, and the blameless will remain in it; but the wicked will be cut off from the land, and the unfaithful will be torn from it."*
> *Proverbs 2:21 & 22 NIV*

The only way we can be upright and blameless is by the Grace of God. Jesus died on the cross to make us upright and blameless. He took the blame for all our sins as if they were His own. He paid the price with His life so that we can remain in the land and not be cut off from it; so that we may learn to be faithful. May we live lives that show the Spirit of Jesus.

Have a Blessed Day! Follow Him! One Less Day to Go!

God blessed me today, when He:

_____

_____

_____

God used me today when I:

_____

_____

_____

I need to ask God to forgive me today for:

_____

_____

_____

JANUARY 13

May the peace of our Lord Jesus Christ be with you!

> "Many deceivers, who do not acknowledge Jesus Christ as coming in the flesh, have gone out into the world. Any such person is the deceiver and the antichrist."
> 2 John 7 NIV

This verse clearly describes the antichrist as anyone who does not "acknowledge Jesus Christ as coming in the flesh." Many so called believers, who call themselves Christians, have not yet come to the place where they truly believe that Jesus is Lord and that He did come as man and died on the cross. Many believe it's just a story made up by the disciples. Many are still waiting on His coming. To acknowledge Jesus Christ as Lord means that we must follow His way 100%. The only way we can do this is by His Grace. May we learn to trust in His power to be obedient to His will.

Have a Blessed Day! Follow Him! One Less Day to Go!

God blessed me today, when He:

_____
_____
_____

God used me today when I:

_____
_____
_____

I need to ask God to forgive me today for:

_____
_____
_____
_____

JANUARY 14

May the peace of our Lord Jesus Christ be with you!

> "But by the grace of God, I am what I am, and His grace to me
> was not without effect. No, I worked harder than all of them –
> yet not I, but the grace of God that was with me."
> 1 Corinthians 15:10 NIV

God's grace is available to all who believe. When we as believers come to the place in our faith in which we know the following: all we are is because of God's grace; we can do nothing without His grace; and we cannot earn His grace…then it is His power that allows us to labor more than we could ever imagine and achieve way beyond our expectations. Then the statement "There go I but for His grace" comes alive and life takes on a whole new perspective. Have you received God's grace?

Have a Blessed Day! Follow Him! One Less Day to Go!

God blessed me today, when He:

_____
_____
_____

God used me today when I:

_____
_____
_____

I need to ask God to forgive me today for:

_____
_____
_____
_____

JANUARY 15

May the peace of our Lord Jesus Christ be with you!

> *"For these commands are a lamp, this teaching is a light, and the corrections of discipline are the way of life."*
> *Proverbs 6:23 NIV*

If we could learn to obey the commandments of the Lord and live according to His will, then we will not stumble. When He disciplines us, He actually saves us from death and Hell. May we all get to know God's commandments and learn to obey. He knows and sees all.

Have a Blessed Day! Follow Him! One Less Day to Go!

God blessed me today, when He:

_____

_____

_____

God used me today when I:

_____

_____

_____

I need to ask God to forgive me today for:

_____

_____

_____

JANUARY 16

May the peace of our Lord Jesus Christ be with you!

> *"Is God the God of Jews only? Is He not the God of Gentiles*
> *too? Yes, of Gentiles too."*
> *Romans 3:29 NIV*

God is the God of all people. True believers know this and share this fact. There are many who will have us believe that God is very selective in who His people are. The devil will try to tempt us into believing that we do not belong to God. But God's word is clear. He is our God. We did not choose Him, He chose us. We did not create Him, He created us. So my brothers and sisters go before your God with confidence that He is your God and you are His people. When all churches, all nations and all races come to accept the fact that there is only one true God and He is our God; then we will have peace on this earth.

Have a Blessed Day! Follow Him! One Less Day to Go!

God blessed me today, when He:

_____
_____
_____

God used me today when I:

_____
_____
_____

I need to ask God to forgive me today for:

_____
_____
_____

JANUARY 17

May the peace of our Lord Jesus Christ be with you!

> *"Restore us, O God Almighty; make Your face shine upon us,*
> *that we may be saved."*
> *Psalm 80:7 NIV*

We have all strayed from the will of God. He is the only one who can restore us to the people He intended us to be...sinless and one with Him. As found in Psalm 51:12, this is a prayer we should pray every day: *Restore 'me' O God Almighty.*

Have a Blessed Day! Follow Him! One Less Day to Go!

God blessed me today, when He:

_____

_____

_____

God used me today when I:

_____

_____

_____

I need to ask God to forgive me today for:

_____

_____

_____

JANUARY 18

May the peace of our Lord Jesus Christ be with you!

> *"To him who overcomes, I will give the right to sit with Me on My throne, just as I overcame and sat down with My Father on His throne."*
> *Revelation 3:21 NIV*

What a promise! But how can we overcome? The truth is we cannot overcome with our own strength. We can only overcome evil thoughts and actions with the help of Jesus. When we surrender our will back to Him, then it is He who overcomes through us. We all have a choice. Connect to the power of the Holy Spirit and defeat evil or succumb to evil. May we all choose to overcome evil by God's grace and take our place with Him.

Have a Blessed Day! Follow Him! One Less Day to Go!

God blessed me today, when He:

_____

_____

_____

God used me today when I:

_____

_____

_____

I need to ask God to forgive me today for:

_____

_____

_____

_____

JANUARY 19

May the peace of our Lord Jesus Christ be with you!

> "This is what the Lord says: "As when juice is still found in a cluster of grapes and men say, 'Don't destroy it, there is yet some good in it,' so will I do in behalf of my servants; I will not destroy them all."
> Isaiah 65:8 NIV

When our Lord comes to judge on that day, will He find "juice" in you and me? Will He count you and me among those that are "yet some good?" If we want to be counted among those who will not be destroyed, we must accept Jesus as Lord and Savior. We must let His Holy Spirit be our guide. May we learn to live according to His will and not our own. Better is one day in His house than thousands elsewhere. Father I pray that You will find some good in all of us. Amen!

Have a Blessed Day! Follow Him! One Less Day to Go!

God blessed me today, when He:

_____
_____
_____

God used me today when I:

_____
_____
_____

I need to ask God to forgive me today for:

_____
_____
_____
_____

JANUARY 20

May the peace of our Lord Jesus Christ be with you!

> *"The righteous man lives a blameless life; blessed are his children after him."*
> *Proverbs 20:7 NIV*

The only perfect and righteous man is Jesus. If we proclaim Him Lord, then we are blessed as His children. We too can live a blameless life when we accept Jesus as Lord and Savior because God does not see our sins anymore. He sees Jesus when He looks at those who have surrendered to Him. Jesus took the blame for all our sins on the cross. Thank You Lord!

Have a Blessed Day! Follow Him! One Less Day to Go!

God blessed me today, when He:

_____
_____
_____

God used me today when I:

_____
_____
_____

I need to ask God to forgive me today for:

_____
_____
_____

JANUARY 21

May the peace of our Lord Jesus Christ be with you!

> *"The disciples, each according to his ability, decided to provide help for the brothers living in Judea."*
> Acts 11:29 NIV

We need to go back to the basics of Christianity. The first Christians took care of one another. They shared and gave "according to his ability." When was the last time you gave according to your ability? When was the last time you: gave a meal to a stranger? mailed a check to a charity? or said a kind word to a stranger? God does not ask us to give more than we are able, just according to our ability. May He inspire us to give according to our abilities and may we be obedient to His instructions.

Have a Blessed Day! Follow Him! One Less Day to Go!

God blessed me today, when He:

_____
_____
_____

God used me today when I:

_____
_____
_____

I need to ask God to forgive me today for:

_____
_____
_____

_____

JANUARY 22

May the peace of our Lord Jesus Christ be with you!

> *"Love must be sincere. Hate what is evil; cling to what is good.*
> *Be devoted to one another in brotherly love. Honor one an-*
> *other above yourselves."*
> *Romans 12:9 & 10 NIV*

This type of love can only come from Jesus. We can only love this way when we have Jesus inside of us because it is now Him who is doing the loving and honoring through us. I pray that you have invited Jesus to come and dwell inside of you. I pray that you fully understand that your body is a temple of the Holy Spirit. What comes out of you is dependent on what is inside of you.

Have a Blessed Day! Follow Him! One Less Day to Go!

God blessed me today, when He:

_____
_____
_____

God used me today when I:

_____
_____
_____

I need to ask God to forgive me today for:

_____
_____
_____

JANUARY 23

May the peace of our Lord Jesus Christ be with you!

> *"But the fruit of the Spirit is love, joy, peace, patience, kindness, goodness, faithfulness, gentleness and self-control. Against such things there is no law."*
> *Galatians 5:22 & 23 NIV*

God's word refers to each of these characteristics as a singular fruit, not many fruits. Is He telling us that we cannot have one without the other? If we are of the Holy Spirit, then we must have all the fruit of the Spirit. We can only achieve this by His Grace. May He fill us with the fruit of His Spirit.

Have a Blessed Day! Follow Him! One Less Day to Go!

God blessed me today, when He:

_____

_____

_____

God used me today when I:

_____

_____

_____

I need to ask God to forgive me today for:

_____

_____

_____

JANUARY 24

May the peace of our Lord Jesus Christ be with you!

> *"During those days men will seek death, but will not find it;*
> *they will long to die, but death will elude them."*
> *Revelation 9:6 NIV*

The book of Revelation is full of horror and destruction. It must be very painful to want to die and not be able to die. We have a choice. We can choose to believe that this is just one man's nightmare, a dream, or we can choose to believe this is God's message to us to be aware. We can be protected from all the destruction to come. All we have to do is accept Jesus as Lord and savior and repent of our sins. Choose wisely brothers and sisters. Choose to believe.

Have a Blessed Day! Follow Him! One Less Day to Go!

God blessed me today, when He:

_____
_____
_____

God used me today when I:

_____
_____
_____

I need to ask God to forgive me today for:

_____
_____
_____

JANUARY 25

May the peace of our Lord Jesus Christ be with you!

> *"How priceless is Your unfailing love! Both high and low among men find refuge in the shadow of Your wings."*
> *Psalm 36:7 NIV*

The loving kindness of our Lord is the only true unconditional loving kindness. Yet we tend to look for loving-kindness elsewhere and we end up broken-hearted and disappointed. May we learn to seek His loving kindness first so that when our fellow men disappoint us, and they will, we always know that we can depend on the Lord!

Have a Blessed Day! Follow Him! One Less Day to Go!

God blessed me today, when He:

_____

_____

_____

God used me today when I:

_____

_____

_____

I need to ask God to forgive me today for:

_____

_____

_____

JANUARY 26

May the peace of our Lord Jesus Christ be with you!

> *"At that very hour there was a severe earthquake and a tenth of the city collapsed. Seven thousand people were killed in the earthquake, and the survivors were terrified and gave glory to the God of Heaven."*
> *Revelation 11:13 NIV*

Why do we wait until there is a disaster to worship God? Even non - believers are known to cry out to God in times of serious danger. The book of Revelation is scary - filled with destruction and pain for non-believers. We who believe should not have to be scared into giving God glory. Worship should be a daily activity, not just a once per week thing to do. May we create a habit of worshiping Him every day.

Have a Blessed Day! Follow Him! One Less Day to Go!

God blessed me today, when He:

_____
_____
_____

God used me today when I:

_____
_____
_____

I need to ask God to forgive me today for:

_____
_____
_____

JANUARY 27

May the peace of our Lord Jesus Christ be with you!

> *"Exalt the Lord our God and worship at His footstool; He is holy."*

> *Psalm 99:5 NIV*

How much time do we spend in exalting and worshipping our God? We all need to spend more time in worship and glorifying our Lord. The Bible is full of guidelines on how we can worship and glorify Him. He is worthy of our worship. He alone is holy. Praise the Lord at all times.

Have a Blessed Day! Follow Him! One Less Day to Go!

God blessed me today, when He:

_____

_____

_____

God used me today when I:

_____

_____

_____

I need to ask God to forgive me today for:

_____

_____

_____

JANUARY 28

May the peace of our Lord Jesus Christ be with you!

> *"I have much to write to you, but I do not want to use paper and ink. Instead, I hope to visit you and talk with you face to face, so that our joy may be complete."*
> *2 John 12 NIV*

If John was writing this today, he might write 'I do not want to use Facebook or texting'. A personal face to face visit; sharing a meal together; listening to the sound of the voice of a loved one; creating another lifetime memory are some of the things that make our joy complete with one another. Please let us not wait until the funeral to spend time with each other. The dead cannot hear or feel anymore. Reach out to a family member, relative or friend today and make your joy complete.

Have a Blessed Day! Follow Him! One Less Day to Go!

God blessed me today, when He:

_____

_____

_____

God used me today when I:

_____

_____

_____

I need to ask God to forgive me today for:

_____

_____

_____

JANUARY 29

May the peace of our Lord Jesus Christ be with you!

> *"Her neighbors and relatives heard that the Lord had shown*
> *her great mercy, and they shared her joy."*
> *Luke 1:58 NIV*

It seems like we tend to share our trials and tribulations more than the mercies we receive from God. When God blesses us He turns sadness and shame to joy. May we learn to share our blessings and rejoice with one another more often. Rejoice with me as one of my best friends of over 30 years accepted Jesus as his Lord and Savior recently. I encourage you to share your blessings. Let us rejoice!

Have a Blessed Day! Follow Him! One Less Day to Go!

God blessed me today, when He:

_____
_____
_____

God used me today when I:

_____
_____
_____

I need to ask God to forgive me today for:

_____
_____
_____

JANUARY 30

May the peace of our Lord Jesus Christ be with you!

> *"If My people, who are called by My name, will humble them-*
> *selves and pray and seek My face and turn from their evil*
> *ways, then I will hear from Heaven and will forgive their sin*
> *and will heal their land."*
> *2 Chronicles 7:14 NIV*

There are so many lessons for us in this verse. First, are you called Christian? Do your family, relatives, friends and co-workers know that you are Christian? What does humility mean to you? Do you ever fall down on your knees before God and pray? Are you determined to "turn from your evil ways?" We who are called Christian must be humble. We must make a greater effort to overcome the temptations of this world and we must pray. Thank God we have Jesus who intercedes for us. May God bless us with humility and strength to turn away from our evil ways.

Have a Blessed Day! Follow Him! One Less Day to Go!

God blessed me today, when He:

_____
_____
_____

God used me today when I:

_____
_____
_____

I need to ask God to forgive me today for:

_____
_____
_____

JANUARY 31

May the peace of our Lord Jesus Christ be with you!

> "The earth is filled with Your love, O Lord; teach me Your decrees."
> Psalm 119:64 NIV

If we could only learn to look for the love of our Lord, that surrounds us. We are always tempted to look for love in strange places and from strange sources. The evil one's mission is to distract us from the truth and the joys of the true love of Jesus. May we learn to focus on God's direction and accept His love with joy.

Have a Blessed Day! Follow Him! One Less Day to Go!

God blessed me today, when He:

_____

_____

_____

God used me today when I:

_____

_____

_____

I need to ask God to forgive me today for:

_____

_____

_____

FEBRUARY 1

May the peace of our Lord Jesus Christ be with you!

> *"Finally, brothers, good-by. Aim for perfection. Listen to my appeal, be of one mind, and live in peace. And the God of love and peace will be with you."*
> *2 Corinthians 13:11 NIV*

This is Paul's wish for us. We serve one God- A God of both love and peace. He alone can make us perfect. He is our comforter. When we all come to the understanding that we are all children of God then we will have peace. Meanwhile, we who believe can learn to live in peace if we could see everyone through the eyes of Jesus. He died for all who would believe.

Have a Blessed Day! Follow Him! One Less Day to Go!

God blessed me today, when He:

_____

_____

_____

God used me today when I:

_____

_____

_____

I need to ask God to forgive me today for:

_____

_____

_____

_____

FEBRUARY 2

May the peace of our Lord Jesus Christ be with you!

> *"Have we not all one Father? Did not one God create us?*
> *Why do we profane the covenant of our fathers by breaking*
> *faith with one another?"*
> *Malachi 2:10 NIV*

When every human being comes to the understanding and belief that we are all God's children, and that means we are all brothers and sisters in His sight, then there will be peace on this earth. May we who believe deal lovingly and kindly with every person we come in contact with. God could be sending certain people to test our faith. May He give us the heart to love His creation.

Have a Blessed Day! Follow Him! One Less Day to Go!

God blessed me today, when He:

_____

_____

_____

God used me today when I:

_____

_____

_____

I need to ask God to forgive me today for:

_____

_____

_____

FEBRUARY 3

May the peace of our Lord Jesus Christ be with you!

> *"I know your deeds. See, I have placed before you an open door that no one can shut. I know that you have little strength, yet you have kept My word and have not denied My name."*
> *Revelation 3:8 NIV*

Our Lord knows everything. He knows what we do and what we do not do; yet He opens the door to Heaven for us. No man or thing can separate us from God as long as we call on His name and keep His word. We must learn to mirror God's word in our actions. Do our thoughts, words and deeds demonstrate our faith?

Have a Blessed Day! Follow Him! One Less Day to Go!

God blessed me today, when He:

_____
_____
_____

God used me today when I:

_____
_____
_____

I need to ask God to forgive me today for:

_____
_____
_____

FEBRUARY 4

May the peace of our Lord Jesus Christ be with you!

> "Jesus answered, "It is written: Man does not live by bread alone, but on every word that come from the mouth of God." Matthew 4:4 NIV

We were created in God's image and God is a Spirit. If we could spend half the time feeding the spirit that we spend feeding the flesh, think about how much spiritually stronger we will be. It takes a strong spirit to overcome the temptations of the devil. So may we feed our bodies, and our spirits. It is the spirit that lasts forever.

Have a Blessed Day! Follow Him! One Less Day to Go!

God blessed me today, when He:

_____

_____

_____

God used me today when I:

_____

_____

_____

I need to ask God to forgive me today for:

_____

_____

_____

FEBRUARY 5

May the peace of our Lord Jesus Christ be with you!

> *"May the God who gives endurance and encouragement give you a spirit of unity among yourselves as you follow Christ Jesus."*
> *Romans 15:5 NIV*

Our Lord sometimes will not deliver us from a trial, but He will give us endurance and encouragement to go through the trouble. He also encourages us to unite as one. That's one good reason to go to church, so we can unite in spirit and voice to praise and honor our Lord. Everyone who has made a commitment to follow Jesus is a member of the Holy Spiritual family. We are brothers and sisters in the faith.

Have a Blessed Day! Follow Him! One Less Day to Go!

God blessed me today, when He:

_____

_____

_____

God used me today when I:

_____

_____

_____

I need to ask God to forgive me today for:

_____

_____

_____

FEBRUARY 6

May the peace of our Lord Jesus Christ be with you!

> *"The Lord will keep you from all harm -- He will watch over your life; the Lord will watch over your coming and going both now and forevermore."*
> *Psalm 121:7 & 8 NIV*

This entire Psalm should be read every day. It is such an encouraging and re-assuring Psalm. Our Lord will keep us from all harm, not just for a certain time but forevermore. May we learn to trust and believe Him, especially when it seems so hard. That's the time He shows His power. May we remember His promises that He will never leave us or forsake us. May we learn to be patient and wait on Him.

Have a Blessed Day! Follow Him! One Less Day to Go!

God blessed me today, when He:

_____
_____
_____

God used me today when I:

_____
_____
_____

I need to ask God to forgive me today for:

_____
_____
_____

_____

FEBRUARY 7

May the peace of our Lord Jesus Christ be with you!

> *"Instead, one of the soldiers pierced Jesus' side with a spear, bringing a sudden flow of blood and water."*
> *John 19:34 NIV*

Our Lord gave everything He had for us, even the last drop of blood. He did not hold back anything. The question we must ask ourselves is am I giving my all to Him or am I holding back anything? You know and He knows. I pray that we who read this will give our all to and for Him.

Have a Blessed Day! Follow Him! One Less Day to Go!

God blessed me today, when He:

_____

_____

_____

God used me today when I:

_____

_____

_____

I need to ask God to forgive me today for:

_____

_____

_____

FEBRUARY 8

May the peace of our Lord Jesus Christ be with you!

"I write these things to you who believe in the name of the Son of God so that you may know that you have eternal life."
1 John 5:13 NIV

This sounds too easy to be true for the logical, worldly mind, but we know that everything is possible with God and His ways are not like the ways of man. If we really believe in Jesus Christ, then we will know for sure that we have eternal life. We must be on guard not to be distracted by the "good" things of this world. The greatest and most precious things of this world are junk when compared to what's waiting in Heaven for us who believe

Have a Blessed Day! Follow Him! One Less Day to Go!

God blessed me today, when He:

_____

_____

_____

God used me today when I:

_____

_____

_____

I need to ask God to forgive me today for:

_____

_____

_____

FEBRUARY 9

May the peace of our Lord Jesus Christ be with you!

> "But the plans of the Lord stand firm forever, the purposes of
> His heart through all generations."
> Psalm 33:11 NIV

We make plans and change them. I am sure you know of people who have already given up on their resolutions for this year. We serve a God who does not make any mistakes. He does not change His mind. He has a plan for you and me. It is a good plan that will never change and will last forever. Now, if we could only be faithful and trust Him. It's His plan and purpose that will come to pass.

Have a Blessed Day! Follow Him! One Less Day to Go!

God blessed me today, when He:

_____

_____

_____

God used me today when I:

_____

_____

_____

I need to ask God to forgive me today for:

_____

_____

_____

FEBRUARY 10

May the peace of our Lord Jesus Christ be with you!

> *"Those whom I love I rebuke and discipline. So be earnest, and repent."*
> *Revelation 3:19 NIV*

True love will not let you destroy yourself. True love will not allow you to go astray. True love will not harm you. God truly loves us. He will not give up on us. He will correct us and discipline us. It is better to be disciplined by a loving Father, than to be a friend of the devil. When He disciplines us let us give thanks and praise.

Have a Blessed Day! Follow Him! One Less Day to Go!

God blessed me today, when He:

_____

_____

_____

God used me today when I:

_____

_____

_____

I need to ask God to forgive me today for:

_____

_____

_____

FEBRUARY 11

May the peace of our Lord Jesus Christ be with you!

> *"May our Lord Jesus Christ Himself and God our Father, who loved us and by His grace gave us eternal encouragement and good hope, encourage your hearts and strengthen you in every good deed and word."*
> *2 Thessalonians 2:16 & 17 NIV*

The things that are happening during these times could be very discouraging for a believer. We must remember that we have a God who loves us and has already given us eternal life with Him. The time we spend on this earth is like a second compared to eternity. This is not it. We have a much better place to look forward to. May we look to Jesus for our encouragement and strength. May we seek His word daily. Our hope is in Jesus and Him only. Do not be discouraged my brothers and sisters. Our Father is in control. Pray for those who do not believe.

Have a Blessed Day! Follow Him! One Less Day to Go!

God blessed me today, when He:

_____

_____

_____

God used me today when I:

_____

_____

_____

I need to ask God to forgive me today for:

_____

_____

_____

FEBRUARY 12

May the peace of our Lord Jesus Christ be with you!

> *"My help comes from the Lord, the Maker of Heaven and Earth."*
> *Psalm 121:2 NIV*

We have the greatest source of power available to us at no cost, yet we try to do things on our own. We choose to do things our way and find ourselves in a mess. Then we fall down on our knees and beg the Lord to rescue us. The good thing is He loves us so much that He will come to rescue us. If we could only learn to go to Him first; think about how much pain and suffering we would not have to endure. Do not be fooled into thinking that anything is too small or too big to bother God about. He is always available and never too busy.

Have a Blessed Day! Follow Him! One Less Day to Go!

God blessed me today, when He:

_____
_____
_____

God used me today when I:

_____
_____
_____

I need to ask God to forgive me today for:

_____
_____
_____

_____

FEBRUARY 13

May the peace of our Lord Jesus Christ be with you!

> *"But if serving the Lord seems undesirable to you, then choose*
> *for yourselves this day whom you will serve, whether the gods*
> *your forefathers served beyond the River, or the gods of the*
> *Amorites, in whose land you are living. But as for me and my*
> *household, we will serve the Lord."*
> *Joshua 24:15 NIV*

Have you made the decision about whom you and your household will serve? Many may say that they do not have any idols in their home, but anything that takes priority over God in our lives could be an idol. Beware of distractions that could take the place of God in your life. It's not about you and me or what we do for God. It's all about God and what He does through us. May we choose to serve our Lord and no other God.

Have a Blessed Day! Follow Him! One Less Day to Go!

God blessed me today, when He:

_____
_____
_____

God used me today when I:

_____
_____
_____

I need to ask God to forgive me today for:

_____
_____
_____

FEBRUARY 14

May the peace of our Lord Jesus Christ be with you!

> *"You, my brothers, were called to be free. But do not use your*
> *freedom to indulge the sinful nature; rather, serve one another*
> *in love."*
> *Galatians 5:13 NIV*

We are the only living being that were given free will to choose. We can choose to succumb to temptations or seek God's help in overcoming the temptations. We need God's help and Spirit to overcome temptations every day. I pray that we will all choose to serve God and love our neighbors as ourselves; every day, not just on Valentine's Day.

Have a Blessed Day! Follow Him! One Less Day to Go!

God blessed me today, when He:

_____

_____

_____

God used me today when I:

_____

_____

_____

I need to ask God to forgive me today for:

_____

_____

_____

FEBRUARY 15

May the peace of our Lord Jesus Christ be with you!

> *"For God so loved the world, that He gave His one and only Son, that whoever believes in Him shall not perish but have eternal life."*
> *John 3:16 NIV*

True love gives and does not expect anything in return. What can you and I give God to show our love for Him compared to what He has done and continues to do for us? We cannot out give God. We can, however, love like Him and give without expecting anything in return. We can feed the poor and comfort the suffering. May we learn to share the love of Jesus by giving our best.

Have a Blessed Day! Follow Him! One Less Day to Go!

God blessed me today, when He:

_____
_____
_____

God used me today when I:

_____
_____
_____

I need to ask God to forgive me today for:

_____
_____
_____

FEBRUARY 16

May the peace of our Lord Jesus Christ be with you!

> *"I am the good shepherd; I know My sheep and My sheep know Me."*
> John 10:14 NIV

There is no doubt that our Lord knows us. He made us. Do we know Him or do we know of Him? There is a big difference. To know of someone is just knowledge. To know someone is to have a personal relationship. How strong is your relationship with Jesus? How often do you talk to Him? How often do you call His name? How often do you talk to others about Him? How obedient are you to His commandments? Building a strong relationship with Jesus is a lifetime process and does not happen in a flash. We are saved by what He did on the cross. It is finished! Let us now build a strong relationship with Jesus. May He really be the Lord of our lives.

Have a Blessed Day! Follow Him! One Less Day to Go!

God blessed me today, when He:

_____
_____
_____

God used me today when I:

_____
_____
_____

I need to ask God to forgive me today for:

_____
_____
_____

FEBRUARY 17

May the peace of our Lord Jesus Christ be with you!

> "He said to them; "You are well aware that it is against our law
> for a Jew to associate with a Gentile or visit him. But God has
> shown me that I should not call any man impure or unclean.""
> *Acts 10:28 NIV*

It is very easy for us to condemn anyone who is different from us.
The difference could be almost anything (race, color, ethnic back-
ground, religious beliefs, sexual preferences etc.). Peter learned that
we should not call any man impure or unclean. None of us have that
right. God is the only true judge. May we learn to leave the judging
up to Him and try our best to please Him in our thoughts, words and
deeds.

Have a Blessed Day! Follow Him! One Less Day to Go!

God blessed me today, when He:

_____
_____
_____

God used me today when I:

_____
_____
_____

I need to ask God to forgive me today for:

_____
_____
_____

_____

FEBRUARY 18

May the peace of our Lord Jesus Christ be with you!

> *"Immediately, something like scales fell from Saul's eyes, and he could see again. He got up and was baptized, and after taking some food he regained his strength.'*
> *Acts 9:18 & 19 NIV*

Saul had to be blinded to all that he believed and did before he could see the truth. The first thing he did was get baptized and accept Jesus as Lord and Savior. Many of us are still blind to the power and saving Grace of Jesus Christ. May we learn to open our eyes and see Jesus everywhere we go. May we all receive the new heart and mind to serve Him and be witnesses for Him just like Paul.

Have a Blessed Day! Follow Him! One Less Day to Go!

God blessed me today, when He:

_____
_____
_____

God used me today when I:

_____
_____
_____

I need to ask God to forgive me today for:

_____
_____
_____

_____

FEBRUARY 19

May the peace of our Lord Jesus Christ be with you!

> *"See, he is puffed up; his desires are not upright - but the righteous will live by His faith."*
> *Habakkuk 2:4 NIV*

What does it mean to live by faith? Where does our faith come from? Many put their faith in the things of this world (jobs, bank accounts with money, other people etc.). Those who believe put their faith in the Lord. The great thing about believing in the Lord is that He actually helps us to be faithful when we give ourselves to Him. May we all learn to live by faith in Jesus.

Have a Blessed Day! Follow Him! One Less Day to Go!

God blessed me today, when He:

_____
_____
_____

God used me today when I:

_____
_____
_____

I need to ask God to forgive me today for:

_____
_____
_____

FEBRUARY 20

May the peace of our Lord Jesus Christ be with you!

> *"He will keep you strong to the end, so that you will be blame-*
> *less on the day of our Lord Jesus Christ."*
> *1 Corinthians 1:8 NIV*

God's promise is that He will keep us strong to the end. So my brothers and sisters when things seem hopeless and you feel helpless, remember that we serve a heavenly Father who keeps us strong and will
present those who believe blameless on the Day of Judgment. Jesus
has already taken all our blame on Himself. Every new day is one day
closer to the "day of our Lord Jesus Christ."

Have a Blessed Day! Follow Him! One Less Day to Go!

God blessed me today, when He:

_____
_____
_____

God used me today when I:

_____
_____
_____

I need to ask God to forgive me today for:

_____
_____
_____

FEBRUARY 21

May the peace of our Lord Jesus Christ be with you!

> *"Those who sow in tears will reap with songs of joy. He who goes out weeping, carrying seed to sow, will return with songs of joy, carrying sheaves with him."*
> *Psalm 126: 5 & 6 NIV*

This is not a perfect world. We who believe will shed many tears as we go through this life. We will be faced with many situations that we do not understand and many people will disappoint us. We must not give up but look to Jesus. Our job is to sow. Jesus will take care of the reaping. Our hope is in Jesus our Savior. Our permanent home is Heaven where we will receive our rewards. May we trust in the Lord and carry our burdens singing His praises.

Have a Blessed Day! Follow Him! One Less Day to Go!

God blessed me today, when He:

_____
_____
_____

God used me today when I:

_____
_____
_____

I need to ask God to forgive me today for:

_____
_____
_____

FEBRUARY 22

May the peace of our Lord Jesus Christ be with you!

> *"Trust in the Lord with all your heart and lean not on your own understanding; in all your ways acknowledge Him, and He will make your paths straight."*
> *Proverbs 3:5&6 NIV*

Many people, believers and non-believers, made resolutions during the past couple weeks. Some have already broken their resolutions. Some have already given up for one reason or another. If we could learn to "trust in the Lord with all our hearts and acknowledge Him," then He will lead us in the right way. We will achieve way beyond our imaginations and capabilities. Let God have His way with you, then watch what He does. You will be amazed.

Have a Blessed Day! Follow Him! One Less Day to Go!

God blessed me today, when He:

_____
_____
_____

God used me today when I:

_____
_____
_____

I need to ask God to forgive me today for:

_____
_____
_____
_____

FEBRUARY 23

May the peace of our Lord Jesus Christ be with you!

> *"For it is not those who hear the law who are righteous in God's sight, but those who obey the law who will be declared righteous."*
> *Romans 2:13 NIV*

Many hear the word and do not believe, and then there are those who hear the word and profess to believe yet do not obey. To believe is to obey. If we believe that Jesus died for our sins, then we will receive the gift of eternal life and obey His law with joy. His grace will empower us to obey because now it is Him who lives in us. Left on our own we will not obey. Thank God that He loves us so much. He gave His life for us to become righteous in God's eyes.

Have a Blessed Day! Follow Him! One Less Day to Go!

God blessed me today, when He:

_____
_____
_____

God used me today when I:

_____
_____
_____

I need to ask God to forgive me today for:

_____
_____
_____

_____

FEBRUARY 24

May the peace of our Lord Jesus Christ be with you!

> *"we know that in all things God works for the good of those who love Him, who have been called according to His purpose."*
> *Romans 8:28 NIV*

It could be a real struggle to believe that "all things work together for good." Especially when we are being tried, tested, and drilled. This is the time when we grow the most. These are the times when we get closer to God. These are the times when our faith becomes stronger and we know how true and sincere our faith is. So brothers and sisters, may we always remember that we worship a Heavenly Father who will not harm us. He will discipline us and teach us. Sometimes we need hard lessons to learn. Trust Him and may your faith be strong. He will never forsake you.

Have a Blessed Day! Follow Him! One Less Day to Go!

God blessed me today, when He:

_____

_____

_____

God used me today when I:

_____

_____

_____

I need to ask God to forgive me today for:

_____

_____

_____

FEBRUARY 25

May the peace of our Lord Jesus Christ be with you!

> *"Do not say, "I'll pay you back for this wrong!" Wait for the
> Lord, and He will deliver you."*
> *Proverbs 20:22 NIV*

It is so easy for us to want to pay back evil for evil. That kind of thinking and action is not from the Lord. It is the devil's way. Our Lord says
to us, that when others hurt us, we should not take things into our
own hands. We should wait on Him. Let Him do what He does best.
He is the only true judge and He alone can save us. So brothers and
sisters, let God have His way because His way is the true and best
way.

Have a Blessed Day! Follow Him! One Less Day to Go!

God blessed me today, when He:

_____

_____

_____

God used me today when I:

_____

_____

_____

I need to ask God to forgive me today for:

_____

_____

_____

_____

FEBRUARY 26

May the peace of our Lord Jesus Christ be with you!

> *"The Lord is exalted, for He dwells on high; He will fill Zion with justice and righteousness. He will be the sure foundation for your times, a rich store for salvation and wisdom and knowledge; the fear of the Lord is the key to this treasure."*
> Isaiah 33:5 &6 NIV

We must learn to exalt our Lord more often. We must learn to respect Him and worship Him in quiet reverence. May we learn to set our hope on Him and seek His wisdom, knowledge and salvation. To obtain these precious gifts we must believe in Him and bow before Him. Do you ever kneel in His presence?

Have a Blessed Day! Follow Him! One Less Day to Go!

God blessed me today, when He:

_____

_____

_____

God used me today when I:

_____

_____

_____

I need to ask God to forgive me today for:

_____

_____

_____

FEABRUARY 27

May the peace of our Lord Jesus Christ be with you!

> *"Give everyone what you owe him: If you owe taxes, pay taxes; if revenue, then revenue; if respect, then respect; if honor, then honor."*
> *Romans 13:7 NIV*

Most of us are getting ready to prepare our taxes. Many are looking for ways not to pay. God's word is specific. We who believe should pay what we owe. This is how we separate ourselves from the non-believer. It can be so hard to respect and honor some people. When you look at another person or do business with another person, what do you see? Try looking at everyone as God's creation - Someone to respect and honor; Someone who needs to hear about the Gospel; Someone who needs to see something different in you; Someone who needs to see the Grace of God.

Have a Blessed Day! Follow Him! One Less Day to Go!

God blessed me today, when He:

_____

_____

_____

God used me today when I:

_____

_____

_____

I need to ask God to forgive me today for:

_____

_____

_____

FEBRUARY 28

May the peace of our Lord Jesus Christ be with you!

> *"What shall I do, Lord?' I asked, 'Get up,' the Lord said, 'and go into Damascus. There you will be told all that you have been assigned to do."'*
> *Acts 22:10 NIV*

What a powerful question, "What shall I do Lord?" If we could only learn to ask God this question before we do anything; just think of how many fewer mistakes we would make! When we ask the question, we must first believe that He will answer. We must then wait on His instructions and obey whatever He tells us to do. He may not, however, tell us everything we want to hear. He told Paul to go to Damascus and there he would be told what to do. Paul obeyed without question. That's the type of faith and obedience God expects from us. May He grant us grace to be faithful and obedient to Him in all things.

Have a Blessed Day! Follow Him! One Less Day to Go!

God blessed me today, when He:

_____

_____

_____

God used me today when I:

_____

_____

_____

I need to ask God to forgive me today for:

_____

_____

_____

FEBRUARY 29 (LEAP YEAR)

May the peace of our Lord Jesus Christ be with you!

> *"Now Thomas, (called Didymus) one of the Twelve, was not*
> *with the disciples when Jesus came."*
> *John 20:24 NIV*

Thomas was not with the disciples at a very critical time. He was not with the disciples when Jesus came. I wonder where he was and what was he doing? We must also ask ourselves, where we will be when Jesus returns? Will He find us among other believers or will we be somewhere else alone? May He find us where He expects us to be. May he find us among other believers.

Have a Blessed Day! Follow Him! One Less Day to Go!

God blessed me today, when He:

_____
_____
_____

God used me today when I:

_____
_____
_____

I need to ask God to forgive me today for:

_____
_____
_____

MARCH 1

May the peace of our Lord Jesus Christ be with you!

> *"These things happened so that the scripture would be ful-filled: "Not one of His bones will be broken," and as another scripture says, "They will look on the one they have pierced.""*
> John 19:36 & 37 NIV

The first coming of Jesus, His life on earth, His crucifixion and resur-rection were all foretold hundreds of years before they happened. The scripture was fulfilled. The second coming has been promised. He will come again (see Acts 1:11). How often do we think of the second coming? We should think about it every day. It's what we as Christians look forward to. May He find us ready and waiting when He comes.

Have a Blessed Day! Follow Him! One Less Day to Go!

God blessed me today, when He:

_____
_____
_____

God used me today when I:

_____
_____
_____

I need to ask God to forgive me today for:

_____
_____
_____

_____

MARCH 2

May the peace of our Lord Jesus Christ be with you!

> *"Lord, Martha said to Jesus, if You had been here, my brother would not have died. But I know that even now God will give you whatever You ask."*
> *John 11:21 & 22 NIV*

If you do not remember the incident of Lazarus, then you should read all of John 11. Martha believed in a physical Jesus. She was not yet exposed to the Spiritual Jesus who is ever present. We are fortunate to know that our Lord is everywhere and never absent. So when we think He is not at our side, He is either in front of us making a clear way for us or behind us pushing us forward. He will never leave us or forsake us. Wherever you are right now He is there. Amen!

Have a Blessed Day! Follow Him! One Less Day to Go!

God blessed me today, when He:

_____

_____

_____

God used me today when I:

_____

_____

_____

I need to ask God to forgive me today for:

_____

_____

_____

_____

MARCH 3

May the peace of our Lord Jesus Christ be with you!

> *"Surely He will save you from the fowler's snare and from the*
> *deadly pestilence."*
> *Psalm 91:3 NIV*

Surely is a definite, it indicates the absence of doubt. Jesus accomplished His mission to save us from the traps of the devil when He died on the cross. We must know that we need Him to save us. If we do not believe we need His saving grace, then we will surely fall into the traps of the devil. May we cry out to our Lord every day to save us from the evil one. We need your saving grace O Lord!

Have a Blessed Day! Follow Him! One Less Day to Go!

God blessed me today, when He:

_____

_____

_____

God used me today when I:

_____

_____

_____

I need to ask God to forgive me today for:

_____

_____

_____

MARCH 4

May the peace of our Lord Jesus Christ be with you!

> "Comfort, comfort My people says your God. Speak tenderly
> to Jerusalem, and proclaim to her that her hard service has
> been completed, that her sin has been paid for, that she has
> received from the Lord's hand double for all her sins."
> Isaiah 40:1 & 2 NIV

We all need comfort from time to time. Our Lord is a God of comfort. He is always available for us to lean on. So my dear brothers and sisters, if you need comfort right now, lean on Jesus. He is able and willing to comfort us. All our sins are paid for and we are pardoned twice as much as we sin. What a Savior!

Have a Blessed Day! Follow Him! One Less Day to Go!

God blessed me today, when He:

_____
_____
_____

God used me today when I:

_____
_____
_____

I need to ask God to forgive me today for:

_____
_____
_____

_____

MARCH 5

May the peace of our Lord Jesus Christ be with you!

> *"For them I sanctify myself, that they too may be truly sanctified."*
> *John 17:19 NIV*

Jesus' mission, goal and focus were always to benefit His brothers and sisters in Christ, His followers. To benefit those who believe in Him and accept Him as Lord and Savior. His every act was for our good. He wants us to be as righteous and holy as He is. The only way we can receive this sanctification is through Him. This is something we receive, not something we can work for or earn. It is a free gift. So let us stretch out our hands and receive the greatest gift that was ever given. As we approach Easter, may we remember that this is a time of celebration of our Lord's victory on the cross.

Have a Blessed Day! Follow Him! One Less Day to Go!

God blessed me today, when He:

_____
_____
_____

God used me today when I:

_____
_____
_____

I need to ask God to forgive me today for:

_____
_____
_____

_____

MARCH 6

May the peace of our Lord Jesus Christ be with you! Sin is NOT our master Jesus is!

> *"But He was pierced for our transgressions, He was crushed for our iniquities; the punishment that brought us peace was upon Him, and by His wounds we are healed."*
> *Isaiah 53:5 NIV*

What Jesus did on the cross was no accident. It was His plan. He intended to pay the price of our sins on the cross. The prophet Isaiah foretold of His suffering, to the minutest detail 400 hundred years before it happened. So as we celebrate Easter, may we remember that we are sinners. We are all in need of the Savior who came and completed the work of taking our place on the cross. When He said His last words on the cross: "It is finished" He meant paid in full. All our sins are paid for if we believe and accept Him as Lord and Savior.

Have a Blessed Day! Follow Him! One Less Day to Go!

God blessed me today, when He:

_____

_____

_____

God used me today when I:

_____

_____

_____

I need to ask God to forgive me today for:

_____

_____

_____

_____

MARCH 7

May the peace of our Lord Jesus Christ be with you!

> *"He has delivered us from such a deadly peril, and He will deliver us again. On Him we have set our hope that He will continue to deliver us."*
> *2 Corinthians 1:10 NIV*

There are many who do not believe that they need deliverance. They will be surprised on the Day of Judgment. We who believe know that Jesus delivered us from sin on the cross. He continues to deliver us even though we continue to sin. Our prayer is that one-day we will sin no more. Thank You Jesus for not giving up on us.

Have a Blessed Day! Follow Him! One Less Day to Go!

God blessed me today, when He:

_____
_____
_____

God used me today when I:

_____
_____
_____

I need to ask God to forgive me today for:

_____
_____
_____

MARCH 8

May the peace of our Lord Jesus Christ be with you!

> *"It was because of the Lord's anger that all this happened to Jerusalem and Judah, and in the end He thrust them from His presence."*
> *Jeremiah 52:3 NIV*

The Lord's anger is a controlled and justified anger. He is also our judge. Jesus received the full force of God's anger on the cross. We are able to come into God's presence because of what Jesus did for us on the cross. When we celebrate Easter, may we focus on the real reason and not forget the pain and suffering. May we remember the moment when the Lord turned away from Jesus as He hung on the cross. He did that for you, all sinners, and me. Thank you Jesus!

Have a Blessed Day! Follow Him! One Less Day to Go!

God blessed me today, when He:

_____
_____
_____

God used me today when I:

_____
_____
_____

I need to ask God to forgive me today for:

_____
_____
_____

_____

MARCH 9

May the peace of our Lord Jesus Christ be with you!

> *"My whole being will exclaim, "Who is like You, O Lord? You rescue the poor from those too strong for them, the poor and needy from those who rob them."*
> *Psalm 35:10 NIV*

Thank God for His power and majesty. We will definitely be defeated by the evil ones if we did not have Him as our shield and defender. May we always remember that we need Him to rescue us and not become complacent. Give thanks for a God who will rescue us.

Have a Blessed Day! Follow Him! One Less Day to Go!

God blessed me today, when He:

_____

_____

_____

God used me today when I:

_____

_____

_____

I need to ask God to forgive me today for:

_____

_____

_____

MARCH 10

May the peace of our Lord Jesus Christ be with you!

> *"He said to him, "If they do not listen to Moses and the Prophets, they will not be convinced even if someone rises from the dead.""*
> *Luke 16:31 NIV*

Moses delivered the 10 Commandments and we have the word of all the prophets and also the Gospels to guide us. Jesus Himself rose from the dead and appeared to many people; yet there are so many who still do not believe. We who believe must not give up on those who do not believe while they live here on earth. It could be very challenging for a believer to understand and accept that there are people who do not believe in Jesus. They exist; so let us continue to share the Gospel because if one unbeliever changes his heart and accepts Jesus as Lord and Savior there will be rejoicing in Heaven.

Have a Blessed Day! Follow Him! One Less Day to Go!

God blessed me today, when He:

_____

_____

_____

God used me today when I:

_____

_____

_____

I need to ask God to forgive me today for:

_____

_____

_____

MARCH 11

May the peace of our Lord Jesus Christ be with you!

> *"'Timothy, guard what has been entrusted to your care. Turn away from Godless chatter and the opposing ideas of what is falsely called knowledge, which some have professed and in so doing have wandered from the faith. Grace be with you.'"*
> *1 Timothy 6:20 & 21 NIV*

We have a responsibility to protect and defend the Gospel. When we converse with others about God and faith, our litmus test must always be, 'Is this of the Lord?' It is very challenging to debate faith and belief. Worldly knowledge can never compete with faith and belief. God's sense is very different from the common sense of man. So let us be on guard and may our knowledge be based on Biblical teachings so that we too will not stray or doubt. 'Grace be with you' is such a powerful benediction. May we receive the grace of our Lord.

Have a Blessed Day! Follow Him! One Less Day to Go!

God blessed me today, when He:

_____
_____
_____

God used me today when I:

_____
_____
_____

I need to ask God to forgive me today for:

_____
_____
_____
_____

MARCH 12

May the peace of our Lord Jesus be with you!

> *"David says the same thing when he speaks of the blessed-ness of the man to whom God credits righteousness apart from works."*
> Romans 4:6 NIV

Too many Christians and churchgoers are still working for their salva-tion. If any one of us could work for our salvation, then Jesus did not have to come and die on the cross for our sins. When we believe that Jesus is Lord and accept Him as Lord and Savior, then the works we do are not so that we will be saved or a sign of gratitude for our salvation. The works we do now are a result of our salvation and it is Jesus who works through us. We are joyful instruments of our Lord. What an hon-or, privilege and humbling experience to be used by The Lord Almighty! Our righteousness comes from the Lord not through our works.

Have a Blessed Day! Follow Him! One Less Day to Go!

God blessed me today, when He:

_____
_____
_____

God used me today when I:

_____
_____
_____

I need to ask God to forgive me today for:

_____
_____
_____
_____

MARCH 13

May the peace of our Lord Jesus Christ be with you!

> *"You show that you are a letter from Christ, the result of our ministry, written not with ink but with the Spirit of the living God, not on tablets of stone but tablets of human hearts."*
> *2 Corinthians 3:3 NIV*

What does your life show? When people interact with you; do they see the image of Jesus Christ. What's in our hearts will influence our words and actions. May our lives be like Jesus and may many non-believers desire to be like us. Our thoughts, words and actions demonstrate the word of God. Remember that!

Have a Blessed Day! Follow Him! One Less Day to Go!

God blessed me today, when He:

_____
_____
_____

God used me today when I:

_____
_____
_____

I need to ask God to forgive me today for:

_____
_____
_____

MARCH 14

May the peace of our Lord Jesus Christ be with you!

"Those controlled by the sinful nature cannot please God."
Romans 8:8 NIV

Who is in control of your mind, body and heart? The things we do; how we behave; our habits; will reveal who is in control: Jesus or the Devil. We who have accepted Jesus as Lord and Savior are free from the control of sin. Jesus is now our Lord and Master. My pastor had us repeat this phrase in church on Sunday, "Sin is not my master." So now whenever I am tempted I repeat the statement, "Sin is not my master." I encourage you to try it and conquer sin.

Have a Blessed Day! Follow Him! One Less Day to Go!

God blessed me today, when He:

_____
_____
_____

God used me today when I:

_____
_____
_____

I need to ask God to forgive me today for:

_____
_____
_____

_____

MARCH 15

May the peace of our Lord Jesus Christ be with you! Sin is not our master.

> *"Who gave Himself for our sins, to rescue us from the present evil age, according to the will of our God and Father, to whom be glory forever and ever, Amen."*
> *Galatians 1:4 & 5 NIV*

Jesus gave Himself for you and me. Nobody did anything to Him without His approval. He did everything according to the will of our Father. The world is still evil and we need deliverance more than ever. May we glorify our Father every day in our thoughts words and actions, because that is the evidence that He is in us.

Have a Blessed Day! Follow Him! One Less Day to Go!

God blessed me today, when He:

_____
_____
_____

God used me today when I:

_____
_____
_____

I need to ask God to forgive me today for:

_____
_____
_____

_____

MARCH 16

May the peace of our Lord Jesus Christ be with you!

> *"..that though the wicked spring up like grass, and all evildo-*
> *ers flourish, they will be forever destroyed. But You O Lord are*
> *exalted forever."*
> *Psalm 92:7 & 8 NIV*

These times are full of evil that seems to just pop up from nowhere. God's word gives us the assurance that their apparent success and growth is for a short time. He will destroy them once and for all. Our Lord always finishes what He starts. Our Father's name will last forever and ever Amen!

Have a Blessed Day! Follow Him! One Less Day to Go!

God blessed me today, when He:

_____

_____

_____

God used me today when I:

_____

_____

_____

I need to ask God to forgive me today for:

_____

_____

_____

_____

MARCH 17

May the peace of our Lord Jesus Christ be with you!

> "No one takes it from Me, but I lay it down of my own ac-
> cord. I have authority to lay it down and authority to take it up
> again. This command I received from My Father."
> John 10:18 NIV

Jesus is the perfect example of power and obedience. He received a command from His Father and carried it out to the end. He knew the source of His power. Our Lord did this for you and me. He did it. No one did it to Him. He gave His life for us. He has the power to die and rise from the dead. Our Lord alone could talk about something like this and then do it. May we also believe that we have access to His power. May we learn to be obedient to our Father.

Have a Blessed Day! Follow Him! One Less Day to Go!

God blessed me today, when He:

_____

_____

_____

God used me today when I:

_____

_____

_____

I need to ask God to forgive me today for:

_____

_____

_____

_____

MARCH 18

May the peace of our Lord Jesus Christ be with you!

> *"I long to see you so that I may impart to you some spiritual gift to make you strong--that is, that you and I may be mutually encouraged."*
> Romans 1:11& 12 NIV

It may sound strange that a man like Paul will need encouragement. But we all do need some encouragement at some time or the other. Have you ever received a phone call, text, or email from a friend at just the right time? We need to encourage one another more often. How about sending your pastor a thank you note? Pick up the phone and call that person who has been on your mind. There is so much we can do to encourage one another. We glorify our Father when He sees His children encouraging one another.

Have a Blessed Day! Follow Him! One Less Day to Go!

God blessed me today, when He:

_____

_____

_____

God used me today when I:

_____

_____

_____

I need to ask God to forgive me today for:

_____

_____

_____

_____

MARCH 19

May the Peace of our Lord Jesus Christ be with you!

> " Many, O Lord my God, are the wonders You have done. The
> things You planned for us no one can recount to You; were I
> to speak and tell of them, they would be too many to declare."
> Psalm 40:5 NIV

We find what we look for. If we look for the wonders that our Lord does
every day, we will find them. If we look for evil, we will find it. So my
brothers and sisters, let us deliberately seek the face of our Lord Jesus
and the wonders He does for us every minute of every day. It is by His
wonder that this verse and words come to you and me every day. Do
not allow the devil to distract us from the wonders that our Lord does
for us every day. Thank you Lord for all the wonders you have done
and continue to do for us. May we never take these things for granted.

Have a Blessed Day! Follow Him! One Less Day to Go!

God blessed me today, when He:

_____

_____

_____

God used me today when I:

_____

_____

_____

I need to ask God to forgive me today for:

_____

_____

_____

MARCH 20

May the peace of our Lord Jesus Christ be with you!

> *"I will remain in the world no longer, but they are still in the world, and I am coming to You. Holy Father, protect them by the power of Your name -- the name You gave Me -- so that they may be one as we are one."*
> *John 17:11 NIV*

Jesus is about to face the most dreadful death of all deaths and whom is He praying for? You and me. Jesus is asking His Father to make us equal to Him and His Father. He gets what He asks for. Do we understand and accept the gifts of protection and oneness with Jesus and God? This is amazing love. Our Lord does not hold anything back. May we learn to accept His protection and power. May we live up to His reputation and understand what it means to be one with God.

Have a Blessed Day! Follow Him! One Less Day to Go!

God blessed me today, when He:

_____
_____
_____

God used me today when I:

_____
_____
_____

I need to ask God to forgive me today for:

_____
_____
_____
_____

MARCH 21

May the peace of our Lord Jesus Christ be with you!

> *"I have set My rainbow in the clouds, and it will be the sign of the covenant between Me and the earth."*
> *Genesis 9:13 NIV*

I saw a complete rainbow in the sky today and it reminded me of God's promises. Read Genesis 9:8-17 to find out more about the exact promise at that time. Since then God has made many promises to those who believe. The rainbow is a sign, a reminder that our God keeps His promises. It is a sign of assurance of our hope in Him. Praise God for His kindness and gentleness to us who are undeserving. The biggest promise was kept on the cross when Jesus died in our place so that we who believe will have eternal life. Thank You Lord for reminding us of Your promises.

Have a Blessed Day! Follow Him! One Less Day to Go!

God blessed me today, when He:

_____
_____
_____

God used me today when I:

_____
_____
_____

I need to ask God to forgive me today for:

_____
_____
_____
_____

MARCH 22

May the peace of our Lord Jesus Christ be with you!

> *"There are different kinds of gifts, but the same Spirit. There*
> *are different kinds of service, but the same Lord."*
> *1 Corinthians 12: 4&5 NIV*

Can you imagine what it would be like if everyone had the same gifts and skills? God, in His wisdom, has blessed each of us with a special talent. All our gifts and talents come from the same source, The Holy Spirit. We all perform different types of service, but we perform for the glory of the Lord. So whatever we do, may we always remember that we serve for the glory of our Lord and not ourselves or to compete with others. Our Lord is not a God of quantity. He is a God of quality and sincerity. He sees and knows all.

Have a Blessed Day! Follow Him! One Less Day to Go!

God blessed me today, when He:

_____
_____
_____

God used me today when I:

_____
_____
_____

I need to ask God to forgive me today for:

_____
_____
_____

MARCH 23

May the peace of our Lord Jesus Christ be with you!

> *"This is a trustworthy saying that deserves full acceptance (and for this we labor); that we have put our hope in the living God, who is the Savior of all men, and especially of those who believe."*
> *1 Timothy 4:9 & 10 NIV*

How should we respond to these two verses? First, we accept them as truth. Second, we make it our work and intent to place our hope in The Living God. Third, we accept Him as Lord and Savior. Good things don't just happen. We serve an engaging God who wants a relationship with us. He will not force Himself on us, but He does promise that if we seek Him we will find Him!

Have a Blessed Day! Follow Him! One Less Day to Go!

God blessed me today, when He:

_____
_____
_____

God used me today when I:

_____
_____
_____

I need to ask God to forgive me today for:

_____
_____
_____

MARCH 24

May the peace of our Lord Jesus Christ be with you!

> *"Be diligent in these matters; give yourself wholly to them, so that everyone may see your progress."*
> *1 Timothy 4:15 NIV*

Are we growing in faith? Is our relationship with Jesus stronger today than it was year ago? Do our family, relatives, co-workers, friends, etc. see a difference in our behavior? We should all conduct a personal progress check up with regards to our spiritual growth and development. Any living organism than ceases to grow begins to die. Too many Christians have reached a point in their walk where they believe that they have arrived. This is a dangerous place to be. Whenever we think we at the peak of our walk the next step starts a downward spiral, may we always look up to Jesus and seek ways to make spiritual progress every day.

Have a Blessed Day! Follow Him! One Less Day to Go!

God blessed me today, when He:

_____
_____
_____

God used me today when I:

_____
_____
_____

I need to ask God to forgive me today for:

_____
_____
_____
_____

MARCH 25

May the peace of our Lord Jesus Christ be with you!

> *"Be strong and courageous. Do not be afraid or discouraged because of the king of Assyria and his vast army with him, for there is a greater power with us than with him."*
> *2 Chronicles 32:7 NIV*

When trials come, and they will in many different forms, we must be strong and courageous and not be afraid. We have the greatest power with us. Too often we get overwhelmed by circumstances and forget that we have a Heavenly Father who is in control and can take care of everything. Call on Him and He will answer.

Have a Blessed Day! Follow Him! One Less Day to Go!

God blessed me today, when He:

_____

_____

_____

God used me today when I:

_____

_____

_____

I need to ask God to forgive me today for:

_____

_____

_____

MARCH 26

May the peace of our Lord Jesus Christ be with you!

> *"So whatever you eat or drink or whatever you do, do it all for the glory of God."*
> *1 Corinthians 10:31 NIV*

We who believe and are Christians must glorify our Father in whatever we do. A good habit is to ask ourselves this question before we take action or say anything: How does this glorify God? We do not work, we glorify God! We do not serve, we glorify God! May every thought, word, and action glorify our Father!

Have a Blessed Day! Follow Him! One Less Day to Go!

God blessed me today, when He:

_____

_____

_____

God used me today when I:

_____

_____

_____

I need to ask God to forgive me today for:

_____

_____

_____

MARCH 27

May the peace of our Lord Jesus Christ be with you!

> *"...and to know this love that surpasses knowledge --that you may be filled to the measure of all the fullness of God."*
> *Ephesians 3:19 NIV*

True love is an everyday activity. The love of God is not a love that can be understood or measured. It is immeasurable and that's how much God loves us. May we not be distracted by chasing after the love of the flesh and miss the most precious love, the love of God.

Have a Blessed Day! Follow Him! One Less Day to Go!

God blessed me today, when He:

_____

_____

_____

God used me today when I:

_____

_____

_____

I need to ask God to forgive me today for:

_____

_____

_____

MARCH 28

May the peace of our Lord Jesus Christ be with you!

> *"God presented Him as a sacrifice of atonement, through faith in His blood. He did this to demonstrate His justice; in His forbearance He had left sins committed beforehand unpunished."*
> *Romans 3:25 NIV*

God presented His only Son Jesus as a sacrifice for you and me. His purpose was to punish sinners, each one of us. Only Jesus could take the place of all us and pay the price of all our sins. What happened on the cross was no accident. It was the result of God's plan. So when we see sin going unpunished, let us remember that God has a plan and know that He will not leave sins committed unpunished. Thank God our sins are already punished.

Have a Blessed Day! Follow Him! One Less Day to Go!

God blessed me today, when He:

_____
_____
_____

God used me today when I:

_____
_____
_____

I need to ask God to forgive me today for:

_____
_____
_____

MARCH 29

May the peace of our Lord Jesus Christ be with you!

> *"And being found in appearance as a man, He humbled Himself and became obedient to death - even death on a cross!"*
> *Philippians 2:8 NIV*

Death on a cross was the most shameful and painful death during the time of Jesus. He chose to die like this for you and me. May we learn to appreciate this every day. May we say, every day, thank you Lord for dying on the cross for me.

Have a Blessed Day! Follow Him! One Less Day to Go!

God blessed me today, when He:

_____
_____
_____

God used me today when I:

_____
_____
_____

I need to ask God to forgive me today for:

_____
_____
_____

MARCH 30

May the peace of our Lord Jesus Christ be with you!

> "Whoever believes in the Son has eternal life, but whoever rejects the Son will not see life, for God's wrath remains on him."
> John 3:36 NIV

The tense used here is present tense. If we believe in Jesus, then we have eternal life. The tense used for those who reject Jesus is for the future, on the day of judgment. We who believe must be more aware of the fact that we have eternal life and our God is not the type who takes back what He has given. No one can fool Him. May we learn to appreciate and enjoy the gift of eternal life.

Have a Blessed Day! Follow Him! One Less Day to Go!

God blessed me today, when He:

_____
_____
_____

God used me today when I:

_____
_____
_____

I need to ask God to forgive me today for:

_____
_____
_____

MARCH 31

May the peace of our Lord Jesus Christ be with you!

> *"At the resurrection people will neither marry nor be given in marriage, they will be like the angels in Heaven."*
> *Matthew 22:30 NIV*

This is a reminder for those who are in great marriages to enjoy each other while you are here on earth. When you get to Heaven things will be different. It could also serve as a consolation for single people. Remember that our time here on earth is short when compared to eternity. The promise for everyone, married or single, is that we will be "like the angels in Heaven."

Have a Blessed Day! Follow Him! One Less Day to Go!

God blessed me today, when He:

_____

_____

_____

God used me today when I:

_____

_____

_____

I need to ask God to forgive me today for:

_____

_____

_____

APRIL 1

May the peace of our Lord Jesus Christ be with you!

> *"When He had received the drink, Jesus said, "It is finished."*
> *With that, He bowed His head and gave up His spirit."*
> *John 19:30 NIV*

"It is finished" are not the words of someone who is giving up. It is a shout of victory. Our Lord finished what He came to do, to die on the cross for your sins and my sins. He was always in control. These words have changed the course of history. With these words He created a way for you and me to come into His presence. We now have a direct line of communication with our Lord. Let us remember that Jesus finished His job. What about us? Our job is to believe and live a life with Him, that reflects His way.

Have a Blessed Day! Follow Him! One Less Day to Go!

God blessed me today, when He:

_____
_____
_____

God used me today when I:

_____
_____
_____

I need to ask God to forgive me today for:

_____
_____
_____

_____

APRIL 2

May the peace of our Lord Jesus Christ be with you!

> *"When they had finished eating, Jesus said to Simon Peter,*
> *"Simon son of John, do you truly love me more than these?"*
> *"Yes, Lord," he said, "you know that I love you." Jesus said,*
> *"Feed My lambs." "*
> *John 21:15 NIV*

What if Jesus should ask you or I, "do you truly love Me?" Can we reply with confidence, "Yes Lord." He knows everything, we cannot fool Him. His command to us, just as it was to Peter is "feed My lambs." So when was the last time you did something good for a stranger, or a poor person, or visited the sick, or prayed with someone who was having a hard time? The answer is an indication of how much we love Jesus. Our Lord expects us to be active for Him. May we be blessed to recognize the opportunities He places in front of us to love Him and give us the courage to follow through.

Have a Blessed Day! Follow Him! One Less Day to Go!

God blessed me today, when He:

_____
_____
_____

God used me today when I:

_____
_____
_____

I need to ask God to forgive me today for:

_____
_____
_____
_____

APRIL 3

May the peace of our Lord Jesus Christ be with you!

> *"Therefore go and make disciples of all nations, baptizing them in the name of the Father and of the Son and of the Holy Spirit, and teaching them to obey everything I have commanded you. And surely I will be with you always, to the very end of the age."*
> *Matthew 28: 19 & 20 NIV*

Let's begin by focusing on Jesus' promise at the end of verse 20. If we believe that He will always be with us, then we will feel His power within us and not hesitate to spread the Gospel. Pray that God will give us vision to recognize every opportunity to share the Gospel and faith. Let us trust that He will equip us with the right words to say. His instruction is to teach them, not beat them up with fear of the consequences of disobedience. The Gospel is all about Jesus sacrificing Himself on the cross to save us from all our sins. This is surely the most precious gift we can share with any one.

Have a Blessed Day! Follow Him! One Less Day to Go!

God blessed me today, when He:

_____
_____
_____

God used me today when I:

_____
_____
_____

I need to ask God to forgive me today for:

_____
_____
_____

APRIL 4

May the peace of our Lord Jesus Christ be with you!

> *The Lord reigns, He is robed in majesty; the Lord is robed in majesty and is armed with strength. The world is firmly established; it cannot be moved.*
> *Psalm 93:1 NIV*

Let us join our hearts, souls, and voices together to proclaim the majesty of our Lord. He is strong. He has created this world and it is well established. I pray that we will be more aware of the majesty and power of our Lord in our daily lives. It is good to reflect on this week and praise and thank Him for His power and majesty. Thank You Lord for all You do to provide for us and protect us.

Have a Blessed Day! Follow Him! One Less Day to Go!

God blessed me today, when He:

_____
_____
_____

God used me today when I:

_____
_____
_____

I need to ask God to forgive me today for:

_____
_____
_____

APRIL 5

May the peace of our Lord Jesus Christ be with you!

> *The salvation of the righteous comes from the Lord; He is their stronghold in time of trouble. The Lord helps them and delivers them; He delivers them from the wicked and saves them, because they take refuge in Him.*
> *Psalm 37:39 & 40 NIV*

Many Christians are being prosecuted today. Some are killed just because of their faith. A believer knows that even in death our Lord rescues us from the enemy. The enemy may think they hurt us when they kill a Christian, but all they are doing is sending us to Heaven to be with our Father. Let us pray for all the Christians, especially in the Middle East, that they will know and believe this verse. When we are faced with trouble; which is promised to us; may we too look to our Lord for help. He is our 'stronghold.'

Have a Blessed Day! Follow Him! One Less Day to Go! HE IS RISEN!

God blessed me today, when He:

_____
_____
_____

God used me today when I:

_____
_____
_____

I need to ask God to forgive me today for:

_____
_____
_____
_____

APRIL 6

May the peace of our Lord Jesus Christ be with you!

> *"This is love for God; to obey His commands. And His commands are not burdensome."*
> *I John 5:3 NIV*

When Jesus gave His life for you and me on the cross He demonstrated the greatest love ever. He also kept His Father's commandments. He said, "Not My will but your will..." (Matthew 26:39). If we love God, we too will keep His commandments and we should know His greatest commandment is to love the Lord your God with all your heart and soul and your neighbor as yourself. When we obey out of love, we obey with joy and no reservations. It is both easy and joyful to obey out of love. Seek to find out how God will have you glorify Him today and everyday then do it with love and joy.

Have a Blessed Day! Follow Him! One Less Day to Go!

God blessed me today, when He:

_____

_____

_____

God used me today when I:

_____

_____

_____

I need to ask God to forgive me today for:

_____

_____

_____

APRIL 7

May the peace of our Lord Jesus Christ be with you!

>*"Make every effort to live in peace with all men (and women)
>and to be holy; without holiness no one will see the Lord."*
>*Hebrews 12:14 NIV*

We are all created in the image of God. Therefore, we should all strive
to reflect His image in all our interactions with everyone. Your face,
kind words, generosity, humility, patience, tolerance and forgiveness
could be the only representations of our Holy Lord that they may experience. We are His body. May others see the holiness of Jesus when
they meet us. Do you want to see Jesus?

Have a Blessed Day! Follow Him! One Less Day to Go!

God blessed me today, when He:

_____

_____

_____

God used me today when I:

_____

_____

_____

I need to ask God to forgive me today for:

_____

_____

_____

_____

APRIL 8

May the peace of our Lord Jesus Christ be with you!

> *"For the Lord will not reject His people; He will never forsake His inheritance."*
> *Psalm 94:14 NIV*

God's people are those who accept Him as Lord and Savior. Those who are obedient to His will. God's people glorify Him in their thoughts, words, and deeds. He will never forsake us. That's His promise and our Lord keeps His promises. If you are feeling lonely and forsaken right now look to the Lord. He is right there beside you. Once we become God's people we are always God's people. If a person used to be a person of God and that person is no longer a believer, then it is that person who has forsaken the Lord and I doubt whether such a person was ever a true person of God. Rejoice in the knowledge that our Lord is with us!

Have a Blessed Day! Follow Him! One Less Day to Go!

God blessed me today, when He:

_____
_____
_____

God used me today when I:

_____
_____
_____

I need to ask God to forgive me today for:

_____
_____
_____
_____

APRIL 9

May the peace of our Lord Jesus Christ be with you!

> *"For God will bring every deed into judgment, including every hidden thing, whether it is good or evil."*
> *Ecclesiastes 12:14 NIV*

Every sinful deed was brought into judgment on the cross and Jesus paid the price with His life. Those who believe and accept Him as Lord and Savior are free from the judgment. Those who do not, will certainly be judged. Nothing can be hidden from God. He sees all and knows all. We who believe have so much to be thankful for. All our sins are forgiven and we can approach our God with a free conscience. Thank You Jesus!

Have a Blessed Day! Follow Him! One Less Day to Go!

God blessed me today, when He:

_____
_____
_____

God used me today when I:

_____
_____
_____

I need to ask God to forgive me today for:

_____
_____
_____

_____

APRIL 10

May the peace of our Lord Jesus Christ be with you! Sin is NOT our master - Jesus is!

> *If a righteous man turns from his righteousness and does evil,*
> *he will die for it. And if a wicked man turns from his wicked-*
> *ness and does what is just and right, he will live by doing so.*
> *Ezekiel 33: 18 & 19 NIV*

We are all sinners who need to turn from our sinful nature and do what is right. We cannot accomplish this on our own. We need the saving grace of our Lord Jesus Christ. If we confess our sins and seek His forgiveness; He will change us from wickedness to what is just and right. He alone can justify us. Let us seek His forgiveness and live a life that is an example of His life.

Have a Blessed Day! Follow Him! One Less Day to Go!

God blessed me today, when He:

_____

_____

_____

God used me today when I:

_____

_____

_____

I need to ask God to forgive me today for:

_____

_____

_____

APRIL 11

May the peace of our Lord Jesus Christ be with you!

Then Jesus told him, "Because you have seen Me, you have believed; blessed are those who have not seen and yet have believed."
John 20:29 NIV

Thomas is known as doubting Thomas. There are many who still do not believe that Jesus died on the cross and rose from the dead,(both religious and non-religious people). Our Lord blesses those who have not seen and yet believe. Do you believe? It would be good to get a response from you as a shout out saying, "I believe!" We are blessed. Do you feel the blessing?

Have a Blessed Day! Follow Him! One Less Day to Go!

God blessed me today, when He:

_____

_____

_____

God used me today when I:

_____

_____

_____

I need to ask God to forgive me today for:

_____

_____

_____

APRIL 12

May the peace of our Lord Jesus Christ be with you!

> *"Then one of them named Caiaphas, who was high priest that year, spoke up, "You know nothing at all. You do not realize that it is better for you that one man die for the people than that the whole nation perish."*
> *John 11:49 & 50 NIV*

This is a great example of the power of the Holy Spirit and how He engineers people to accomplish His plan. Caiaphas did not know anything. He was being used by God to get the Jews of that time to plot to kill Jesus. This is exactly what Jesus wanted. He came to die for all of us. Our God is alive and in control even when it looks like He is not. That's our faith and trust.

Have a Blessed Day! Follow Him! One Less Day to Go!

God blessed me today, when He:

_____
_____
_____

God used me today when I:

_____
_____
_____

I need to ask God to forgive me today for:

_____
_____
_____

APRIL 13

May the peace of our Lord Jesus Christ be with you!

> *"Early in the morning they left for the Desert of Tekoa. As they set out, Jehosaphat stood and said, "Listen to me, Judah and people of Jerusalem! Have faith in the Lord your God and you will be upheld; have faith is His prophets and you will be successful."*
> *2 Chronicles 20:20 NIV*

Believe is an action word. Our beliefs impact our decisions which in turn impact the actions we take or not take; which then impact the results we achieve or not achieve; and in turn validate what we believed in the first place. We go through this cycle several times every day and sometimes we get disappointed. The only one who will never let us down is our God. We believe in Him as if He has already done what we believe He will do. That's real belief. May we learn to believe in our Lord as if he has already provided and then wait on Him.

Have a Blessed Day! Follow Him! One Less Day to Go!

God blessed me today, when He:

_____
_____
_____

God used me today when I:

_____
_____
_____

I need to ask God to forgive me today for:

_____
_____
_____
_____

APRIL 14

May the peace of our Lord Jesus Christ be with you!

> *"The earth is the Lord's, and everything in it, the world, and all who live in it."*
> *Psalm 24:1 NIV*

People all over the world are fighting for territory. They claim land as if it is their own. When everyone comes to the understanding and belief that the world belongs to the Lord and not man, then we will have peace. God owns everything. I have never been to a funeral where they place the deed or title for property in the coffin. Look around you. Look up, look down. Everything you see belongs to the Lord. May we acknowledge God's sovereignty and His grace to allow us the privilege to enjoy His land while we live here. Thank you Lord!

Have a Blessed Day! Follow Him! One Less Day to Go!

God blessed me today, when He:

_____
_____
_____

God used me today when I:

_____
_____
_____

I need to ask God to forgive me today for:

_____
_____
_____
_____

APRIL 15

May the peace of our Lord Jesus Christ be with you!

> *"And I – in righteousness I will see Your face; when I awake, I will be satisfied with seeing Your likeness."*
> *Psalm 17:15 NIV*

The Lord is righteous in all His dealings with us. He is always righteous; not sometimes. Our God is not a convenient God. We need to be more aware of His righteousness. The righteous that Jesus made available for us when He died on the cross. When we sacrifice our bodies with Jesus we too will arise with a new righteous body that is in the image of our Lord. We will be restored to the original creation. That is our hope.

Have a Blessed Day! Follow Him! One Less Day to Go!

God blessed me today, when He:

_____
_____
_____

God used me today when I:

_____
_____
_____

I need to ask God to forgive me today for:

_____
_____
_____

APRIL 16

May the peace of our Lord Jesus Christ be with you!

> "He got up, rebuked the wind and said to the waves, "Quiet!
> Be still!" Then the wind died down and it was completely calm."
> Mark 4:39 NIV

Our Lord is in control of everything. Even nature obeys His command. The question we need to ask ourselves is why do we have such a hard time obeying His command? Note that "the wind died down and it was completely calm." When Jesus does something He goes all the way, completely. He does not bless us with half of a blessing. When He provides our cup runs over. So whatever is troubling you, whatever storms you may be facing, know that Jesus can completely resolve the situation. Our role is to have faith and trust Him.

Have a Blessed Day! Follow Him! One Less Day to Go!

God blessed me today, when He:

_____
_____
_____

God used me today when I:

_____
_____
_____

I need to ask God to forgive me today for:

_____
_____
_____
_____

APRIL 17

May the peace of our Lord Jesus Christ be with you!

> "Such a high priest meets our need-- one who is holy, blameless, pure, set apart from sinners, exalted above the Heavens." Hebrews 7:26 NIV

The writer of Hebrews uses clear and exact words to describe Jesus who is also our high priest. In fact, He is the highest of all. He has the qualities that we need to aspire to achieve. We too are able to be like Him, if we let Him have His way with us. When we respond to His knock and let Him into our lives it is His holiness, His purity that equips us to be set apart from sinning. May we glorify and worship our high Priest with joy and pride.

Have a Blessed Day! Follow Him! One Less Day to Go!

God blessed me today, when He:

_____

_____

_____

God used me today when I:

_____

_____

_____

I need to ask God to forgive me today for:

_____

_____

_____

_____

APRIL 18

May the peace of our Lord Jesus Christ be with you!

> *"And whatever you do, whether in word or deed, do it all in the name of the Lord Jesus, giving thanks to God the Father through Him."*
> *Colossians 3:17 NIV*

Our words and our deeds either glorify God or the devil. There is no third person. Our thoughts, words and actions will glorify God when we surrender ourselves to Him. The amazing thing about our Lord is that He knows all. If we ask Him to guide us, He will. We must remember to give Him thanks for all He equips us to do. Please know that without His help and Holy Spirit we are doomed. When we are filled with His power we can do all things to His glory.

Have a Blessed Day! Follow Him! One Less Day to Go!

God blessed me today, when He:

_____

_____

_____

God used me today when I:

_____

_____

_____

I need to ask God to forgive me today for:

_____

_____

_____

_____

APRIL 19

May the peace of our Lord Jesus Christ be with you!

> "But our citizenship is in Heaven. And we eagerly await a
> Savior from there, the Lord Jesus Christ, who by the power
> that enables Him to bring everything under His control, will
> transform our lowly bodies so that they will be like His glori-
> ous body."
> Philippians 3:20 & 21 NIV

Any attempt to change our vile body without the intervention of our
Lord Jesus is futile. It will fail. He alone can restore us to the original
creation, in His image. He has the genuine blueprint; He has the
power, no one else; and He has the desire. So my dear brothers and
sisters may we seek Him every day. May we have conversations with
Him and listen to His instructions.

Have a Blessed Day! Follow Him! One Less Day to Go!

God blessed me today, when He:

_____

_____

_____

God used me today when I:

_____

_____

_____

I need to ask God to forgive me today for:

_____

_____

_____

APRIL 20

May the peace of our Lord Jesus Christ be with you!

"I have much more to say to you, more than you can now bear. But when He, the Spirit of truth, comes, He will guide you into all truth. He will not speak on His own; He will speak only what He hears, and He will tell you what is to come."
John 16:12&13 NIV

Our Lord knows everyone of us. He knows our strengths and our weaknesses. He will feed us according to what we need in the moment. He will never give us too much to overwhelm or confuse us. He provides enough at this time. Let us be content with what He reveals to us and be patient knowing that He will feed us according to our capacity to receive His word. One day we will be just like Him in Heaven, all knowing. Right now let us give thanks for what He tells us.

Have a Blessed Day! Follow Him! One Less Day to Go!

God blessed me today, when He:

_____
_____
_____

God used me today when I:

_____
_____
_____

I need to ask God to forgive me today for:

_____
_____
_____

APRIL 21

May the peace of our Lord Jesus Christ be with you!

"Therefore, whoever humbles himself like this child is the greatest in the kingdom of Heaven."
Matthew 18:4 NIV

To humble ourselves is a choice. Pride leads to destruction and is not of the Lord. Jesus humbled Himself when He came as man into this world and He died the most humiliating death on the cross. He washed His disciples' feet. This is our Lord and Master, the God of all Gods. If we proclaim to be His followers, then we too must choose to humble ourselves. This will cause some pain and suffering, but that's the promise of our Lord. He also promises that we who humble ourselves like a child are "the greatest in the kingdom of Heaven." Our life in Heaven is so much more important and everlasting compared to our lives here on Earth.

Have a Blessed Day! Follow Him! One Less Day to Go!

God blessed me today, when He:

_____

_____

_____

God used me today when I:

_____

_____

_____

I need to ask God to forgive me today for:

_____

_____

_____

_____

APRIL 22

May the peace of our Lord Jesus Christ be with you!

> "Be shepherds of God's flock that is under your care, serving
> as overseers -- not because you must, but because you are
> willing, as God wants you to be; not greedy for money, but
> eager to serve, not lording it over those entrusted to you, but
> being examples to the flock."
> 1 Peter 5:2 & 3 NIV

God will provide opportunities for all of His children to serve others.
Some of us may get one person to serve, while others may get many.
God is not a God of numbers. He will reward us based on the level
of service and the unselfish heart with which we serve. We are His
stewards; His helpers; His hands and feet. We must be available and
willing when He calls upon us to be a shepherd to another person.
May we recognize the people God place in our lives to serve and
willingly serve with joy!

Have a Blessed Day! Follow Him! One Less Day to Go!

God blessed me today, when He:

_____

_____

_____

God used me today when I:

_____

_____

_____

I need to ask God to forgive me today for:

_____

_____

_____

_____

APRIL 23

May the peace of our Lord Jesus Christ be with you!

> *"He called a little child and had him stand among them. And He said; "I tell you the truth, unless you change and become like little children, you will never enter the Kingdom of Heaven."*
> *Matthew 18:2 NIV*

This was our Lord's answer to the disciples question "Who is the greatest in the kingdom of Heaven?" vs 1. Note how Jesus was specific about 'little children.' He even used an example of a 'little child.' The Bible does not tell us how old this child was, but it does say that it was a little child. What does it mean to be 'like a little child.' Next time you are in the presence of a little child, note how non-judgmental he or she is. Note how they play with one another. They are not concerned about color of skin, ethnic origin, the clothes the other child is wearing etc. They just want to love one another. We need to 'change and become like little children' if we want to go to Heaven.

Have a Blessed Day! Follow Him! One Less Day to Go!

God blessed me today, when He:

_____

_____

_____

God used me today when I:

_____

_____

_____

I need to ask God to forgive me today for:

_____

_____

_____

APRIL 24

May the peace of our Lord Jesus Christ be with you!

> *"Let them give thanks to the Lord for His unfailing love and*
> *His wonderful deeds for men."*
> Psalm 107:32 NIV

We have so much to give thanks to the Lord! But His "unfailing love"
is the most precious. God loves us with a love that never fails. His
love for us in unconditional. May we give Him thanks for His love for
us every day.

Have a Blessed Day! Follow Him! One Less Day to Go!

God blessed me today, when He:

_____

_____

_____

God used me today when I:

_____

_____

_____

I need to ask God to forgive me today for:

_____

_____

_____

APRIL 25

May the peace of our Lord Jesus Christ be with you!

> *"He who descended is the very One who ascended higher than all the Heavens, in order to fill the whole universe."*
> *Ephesians 4:10 NIV*

The crucifixion of Jesus Christ on the cross; His death and His resurrection is no fairy tale. These things really happened. Our Lord did go to Hell and rose victorious. We too sometimes will feel as if we have descended to a low point of our lives, and that will happen. When we feel this way, let us remember that, like Jesus we too can rise again by the power of His Grace. Our Lord has the power to reach us wherever we are, and lift us up. His plan is to lift us up with Him.

Have a Blessed Day! Follow Him! One Less Day to Go!

God blessed me today, when He:

_____

_____

_____

God used me today when I:

_____

_____

_____

I need to ask God to forgive me today for:

_____

_____

_____

APRIL 26

May the peace of our Lord Jesus Christ be with you!

> *"As you know, we consider blessed those who have perse-*
> *vered. You have heard of Job's perseverance, and have seen*
> *what the Lord finally brought about. The Lord is full of com-*
> *passion and mercy."*
> James 5:11 NIV

Perseverance is a blessing that comes from strong faith in the Lord. Job lost everything, but he never stopped trusting and believing in the Lord. The Lord returned everything Job lost times 3. Many of us may never see a reward for our perseverance on this earth. Our reward is in Heaven. If we truly believe that Heaven is real then we will persevere.

Our Father will never give up on us. Let us hold on to Him and never give up. A mansion is waiting for each of us in Heaven.

Have a Blessed Day! Follow Him! One Less Day to Go!

God blessed me today, when He:

_____

_____

_____

God used me today when I:

_____

_____

_____

I need to ask God to forgive me today for:

_____

_____

_____

APRIL 27

May the peace of our Lord Jesus Christ be with you!

> *"In God I trust; I will not be afraid. What can man do to me?"*
> *Psalm 56:11 NIV*

Trust is the key ingredient to every relationship; no matter what your belief may be. When trust breaks down, the relationship falls apart. Our God is the only one we can really trust. He will never let us down. He will never forsake us. His love is unconditional and everlasting. We can trust Him 100% to protect us from every danger. That does not mean that we will not extend trust to our fellow believers, but we must be smart about who we trust.

Have a Blessed Day! Follow Him! One Less Day to Go!

God blessed me today, when He:

_____

_____

_____

God used me today when I:

_____

_____

_____

I need to ask God to forgive me today for:

_____

_____

_____

APRIL 28

May the peace of our Lord Jesus Christ be with you!

> *"His splendor was like the sunrise; rays flashed from His hand,*
> *where His power was hidden."*
> *Habakkuk 3:4 NIV*

What a vivid description of the glory of our Lord! May we use this verse as a reminder of the greatness of our Lord. We seem to be so busy taking care of daily duties and responsibilities that we neglect to focus on the glory of our Lord. He is all around us and above us. Look around and above my brothers and sisters and adore our glorious Father.

Have a Blessed Day! Follow Him! One Less Day to Go!

God blessed me today, when He:

_____
_____
_____

God used me today when I:

_____
_____
_____

I need to ask God to forgive me today for:

_____
_____
_____

APRIL 29

May the peace of our Lord Jesus Christ be with you!

> "He chose to be mistreated along with the people of God,
> rather than to enjoy the pleasures of sin for a short time."
> Hebrews 11:25 NIV

Every one of us makes choices everyday - believers and non-believers. God created us in His image and gave us free will. There are many references to men and women of the Bible who made choices that were not popular with the world. But they decided to choose a life obedient to the Lord rather than a life in the luxury of this world. When we are faced with choices; may we be like Moses and make the choices that will please and glorify our Heavenly Father. He will reward us with treasures that our present minds cannot even imagine. Choose wisely my brothers and sisters. We will either enjoy the benefits of the choices we make or suffer the consequences.

Have a Blessed Day! Follow Him! One Less Day to Go!

God blessed me today, when He:

_____
_____
_____

God used me today when I:

_____
_____
_____

I need to ask God to forgive me today for:

_____
_____
_____

APRIL 30

May the peace of our Lord Jesus Christ be with you!

> "...and receive from Him anything we ask, because we obey
> His commands and do what pleases Him. And this is His com-
> mand: to believe in the name of His Son, Jesus Christ, and to
> love one another as He commanded us."
> 1 John 3:22 & 23 NIV

Christianity is the simplest religion. All we have to do to please our God (the one and only God) is to believe in Jesus Christ and love one another. We are the ones who tend to complicate matters. Let's be obedient by sticking to His commands and not add any of our own. When we believe in Jesus Christ we will only ask for things that please and glorify Him. Ask and believe that He will provide. Remember we are His children.

Have a Blessed Day! Follow Him! One Less Day to Go!

God blessed me today, when He:

_____

_____

_____

God used me today when I:

_____

_____

_____

I need to ask God to forgive me today for:

_____

_____

_____

MAY 1

May the peace of our Lord Jesus Christ be with you!

>*"Humble yourselves therefore under God's mighty hand, that*
>*He may lift you up in due time."*
>*1 Peter 5:6 NIV*

It looks like humility is a recurring theme this week. God must want us to be more humble. Pride seeks the approval of man. Humility will receive the approval of our Lord. If we are humble, we may never be exalted in this life, but in God's time, He will exalt us. So let us pray that He will fill us with His Holy Spirit to humble ourselves in all that we say and do.

Have a Blessed Day! Follow Him! One Less Day to Go!

God blessed me today, when He:

_____

_____

_____

God used me today when I:

_____

_____

_____

I need to ask God to forgive me today for:

_____

_____

_____

MAY 2

May the peace of our Lord Jesus Christ be with you!

> *"You did not choose Me, but I chose you to go and bear fruit*
> *- fruit that will last. Then the Father will give you whatever you*
> *ask in My name. This is My command: Love one another."*
> *John 15: 16 & 17 NIV*

Our Lord Jesus chose you and me for a purpose "to go and bear fruit." We are offered many opportunities every day to bare fruit, to show God's love and kindness to the people He places in our space. May we always be on the alert and recognize these opportunities then respond as the Holy Spirit leads us. Look at the unlimited reward He offers in return – "Then My Father will give you whatever you ask in My name." This is followed by a *command* to love one another, which indicates that loving one another could be the most precious fruit. So may our thoughts, words, and actions be full of love for one another.

Have a Blessed Day! Follow Him! One Less Day to Go!

God blessed me today, when He:

_____
_____
_____

God used me today when I:

_____
_____
_____

I need to ask God to forgive me today for:

_____
_____
_____
_____

MAY 3

May the peace of our Lord Jesus Christ be with you!

> *"God is our refuge and strength, an ever present help in trouble."*
> *Psalm 46:1 NIV*

We worship the God who is always with us in good times and bad times. The Psalmist does not say in times of big trouble. He says in times of trouble. We sometimes fail to go before our Lord in times of small troubles by fooling ourselves into thinking we can take care of this little thing. We fool ourselves by thinking this is too small to bother God. And when the one little thing becomes big we cry out to the Lord. This is not how our Lord works. He is always present in times of all kinds and sizes of trouble. Let us thank Him that He chooses to be with us and let us be aware that He is with us; not just as an observer; but a Divine helper.

Have a Blessed Day! Follow Him! One Less Day to Go!

God blessed me today, when He:

_____

_____

_____

God used me today when I:

_____

_____

_____

I need to ask God to forgive me today for:

_____

_____

_____

MAY 4

May the peace of our Lord Jesus Christ be with you!

> *"If anyone's name was not found written in the book of life, he was thrown into the lake of fire."*
> *Revelation 20: 15 NIV*

Is your name written in the book of life? If it is, you will know for sure and you will have an assurance that only comes from the Lord. How does a person's name get written in the book of life? There is only one way, through faith and belief in Jesus Christ. If you are not sure whether your name is written in the book of life, pray the sinner's prayer:

"Dear God, I know that I am a sinner. I know that my sin deserves to be punished. I believe Christ died for me and rose from the grave. I trust Jesus Christ alone as my Savior. Thank you for the forgiveness and everlasting life I now have. In Jesus' name, Amen."

Have a Blessed Day! Follow Him! One Less Day to Go!

God blessed me today, when He:

_____

_____

God used me today when I:

_____

_____

I need to ask God to forgive me today for:

_____

_____

_____

MAY 5

May the peace of our Lord Jesus Christ be with you!

> *"He who has an ear, let him hear what the Spirit says to the churches."*
> Revelation 3:22 NIV

This verse also appears in Revelation 2:29 and 3: 13, therefore it must be important. We all have ears that hear, but do we listen to what the Spirit says? The difference between listening and hearing is choice. We choose to listen and when we listen we take action. May we choose to listen to our Heavenly Father and obey His commandments. To listen to Jesus we must find a quiet place and remove all the distractions of this world. Note how many times Jesus went to a garden when He wanted to pray. Quiet time with Jesus is precious.

Have a Blessed Day! Follow Him! One Less Day to Go!

God blessed me today, when He:

_____

_____

_____

God used me today when I:

_____

_____

_____

I need to ask God to forgive me today for:

_____

_____

_____

MAY 6

May the peace of our Lord Jesus Christ be with you!

> "No one can serve two masters. Either he will hate the one and love the other, or he will be devoted to the one and despise the other. You cannot serve both God and Money." Matthew 6:24 NIV

This is a very well-known verse. Note that money begins with a capital letter 'M' in the NIV indicating that it's more than just the material wealth. It's the devil at work when he tries to bribe us with money. The irony is that the money comes from God. Zig Ziglar once said, "It's ok to have money. It's when the money has you then you are in big trouble." So let us pray that no amount of money will separate us from God and that we will always place Him first in our lives.

Have a Blessed Day! Follow Him! One Less Day to Go!

God blessed me today, when He:

_____

_____

_____

God used me today when I:

_____

_____

_____

I need to ask God to forgive me today for:

_____

_____

_____

_____

MAY 7

May the peace of our Lord Jesus Christ be with you!

> *"For the revelation awaits an appointed time; it speaks of the end and will not prove false. Though it linger, wait for it; it will certainly come and will not delay."*
> *Habakkuk 2: 3 NIV*

Our Lord has made many revelations. The entire book of Revelations is mostly about them. We must remember that God's time is different from our time. His time is the real time and correct time. Our role is to be faithful and wait, knowing that it will come to pass. Every promise will come to pass in God's time. Meanwhile we walk by faith. Note: we walk, not stand still. We continue living in faith and do what our Lord commands us. We continue trusting that His revelations will come to pass. Our Lord is in control of all things.

Have a Blessed Day! Follow Him! One Less Day to Go!

God blessed me today, when He:

_____

_____

_____

God used me today when I:

_____

_____

_____

I need to ask God to forgive me today for:

_____

_____

_____

MAY 8

May the peace of our Lord Jesus Christ be with you!

"For God did not call us to be impure, but to live a holy life."
1 Thessalonians 4:7 NIV

We who have responded in a positive way to the call of Jesus and have accepted Him as Lord and Savior are now cleansed from sin by His blood. For a better understanding of what it means to be unclean, read 1 Thessalonians chapter 4: 1 to 12.We have a Savior who can and will protect us from all temptation if we call upon Him. Our Lord is restoring us to His original creation, in His image and sinless. In other words, holy like Him. Thank You Lord!

Have a Blessed Day! Follow Him! One Less Day to Go!

God blessed me today, when He:

_____
_____
_____

God used me today when I:

_____
_____
_____

I need to ask God to forgive me today for:

_____
_____
_____

MAY 9

May the peace of our Lord Jesus Christ be with you!

> "Moreover, I will give you what you have not asked for--both riches and honor--so that in your lifetime you will have no equal among kings. And if you walk in My ways and obey My statutes and commands, as David your father did, I will give you long life."
> 1 Kings 3:13 & 14 NIV

When we pray, what do we ask for? Most times we ask for matters of the flesh. May we learn from King Solomon and ask for what pleases God. Then the Lord will bless us with what we ask for and even some things we do not ask for. Have you ever received a blessing that you never expected or even thought you deserved? That's God's grace at work. Note the warning of verse 14, "...if you walk in My ways and obey My statutes and commands ... I will give you long life." We receive so much from the Lord that we do not ask for, and do not deserve. Yet we are missing out on so much more if we do not ask for what pleases Him. May we seek to please Him in all that we do.

Have a Blessed Day! Follow Him! One Less Day to Go!

God blessed me today, when He:

_____

_____

God used me today when I:

_____

_____

I need to ask God to forgive me today for:

_____

_____

_____

MAY 10

May the peace of our Lord Jesus Christ be with you!

> *But you have an anointing from the Holy One, and all of you*
> *know the truth.*
> *1 John 2:20 NIV*

Those who believe and have accepted Jesus as Lord and Savior are anointed with His blood. We are blessed with the revelation of God's word, which is the truth as revealed in the Holy Bible. To know and believe demands that we take action. Our action is to share the truth with those who the Lord places in our presence. May we be on the lookout for those who do not know the truth and trust God to equip us to share His truth. Let us be intentional about sharing the truth.

Have a Blessed Day! Follow Him! One Less Day to Go!

God blessed me today, when He:

_____

_____

_____

God used me today when I:

_____

_____

_____

I need to ask God to forgive me today for:

_____

_____

_____

MAY 11

May the peace of our Lord Jesus Christ be with you!

> *And over all these virtues put on love, which binds them all together in perfect unity.*
> *Colossians 3:14 NIV*

A true Christian who is dead to sin and lives the life of the new risen man or woman will live a life that's full of love, see verses 10 to 17 for more guidelines on the saved live.

May we always be mindful of what pleases God and live a life that exemplifies the risen Savior. Meditate on these instructions and make a determined choice to live this way. The Holy Spirit inside of us will empower us to live a life like this. We cannot do it on our own. We need Jesus.

Have a Blessed Day! Follow Him! One Less Day to Go!

God blessed me today, when He:

_____

_____

_____

God used me today when I:

_____

_____

_____

I need to ask God to forgive me today for:

_____

_____

_____

MAY 12

May the peace of our Lord Jesus Christ be with you!

> *"That is why, for Christ's sake, I delight in weaknesses, in insults, in hardships, in persecutions, in difficulties. For when I am weak, then I am strong."*
> 2 Corinthians 12:10 NIV

If we know the story of Paul, then we know how much pain and suffering he experienced in his lifetime. We wonder how he could have taken pleasure in all of this. Paul knew that these trials and tribulations created a greater appreciation and need for Jesus. He also knew that being a Christian brings persecution, which is a confirmation and validation that you are a Christian. That's how Paul can rejoice in his sufferings for Christ's sake. May we too be like Paul and take pleasure when we are persecuted for Christ's sake. It's time to take a stand and let the world know that we are Christian. Our Lord will protect us and fill us with His power to become strong.

Have a Blessed Day! Follow Him! One Less Day to Go!

God blessed me today, when He:

_____
_____
_____

God used me today when I:

_____
_____
_____

I need to ask God to forgive me today for:

_____
_____
_____
_____

MAY 13

May the peace of our Lord Jesus Christ be with you!

> *"All the ends of the earth will remember and turn to the Lord,*
> *and all the families of the nations will bow down before Him."*
> *Psalm 22:27 NIV*

If we read or watch the news on TV, it would appear as if we are losing the battle. Nations are turning away from the commands of the Lord. Religions are compromising the word. Many Christians are being killed because of their faith. We cannot give up hope because God is all-powerful and the Psalmist reminds us that all nations shall turn back to the Lord and worship Him. Let us be strong and steadfast in our faith and not give up. The battle is already won. We worship a victorious God.

Have a Blessed Day! Follow Him! One Less Day to Go!

God blessed me today, when He:

_____

_____

_____

God used me today when I:

_____

_____

_____

I need to ask God to forgive me today for:

_____

_____

_____

_____

MAY 14

May the peace of our Lord Jesus Christ be with you!

> *"…remember this; whoever turns a sinner from the error of his way will save him from death and cover over a multitude of sins."*
> *James 5:20 NIV*

Our tendency is to point out the sins of our fellow man. We ignore the sinner and shy away from their presence. Our Lord wants us to help the sinner to confess their sins and repent. Our job is to introduce them to Jesus, the only one who can save them from death. We cannot do this from afar. We need to draw beside the sinner and gain their trust. We need to make our intentions clear. All we want to do is introduce you to Jesus and let Him have His way. Let us pray that the Lord will use us to save more sinners from death. One of my own greatest concerns is that I will get to Heaven and look down in hell and see someone I knew who I did not introduce to Jesus. Lord open our eyes to see those who need you and give us the power to draw them to you.

Have a Blessed Day! Follow Him! One Less Day to Go!

God blessed me today, when He:

_____

_____

_____

God used me today when I:

_____

_____

_____

I need to ask God to forgive me today for:

_____

_____

_____

MAY 15

May the peace of our Lord Jesus Christ be with you!

> *"And He took bread, gave thanks and broke it, and gave it to them, saying, "This is My body given for you; do this in remembrance of Me.""*
> *Luke 22:19 NIV*

Memorial Day is a holiday in the United States. Many people will spend some time remembering the soldiers who gave their lives in battle. Our Lord gave His life for us on the cross. He wants us to remember Him. The Sacrament of Holy Communion is a time to remember what Jesus did for us and His relationship with us. Every day is Memorial Day in the life of a Christian. May we never forget what our Lord has done and continues to do for us.

Have a Blessed Day! Follow Him! One Less Day to Go!

God blessed me today, when He:

_____

_____

_____

God used me today when I:

_____

_____

_____

I need to ask God to forgive me today for:

_____

_____

_____

MAY 16

May the peace of our Lord Jesus Christ be with you!

> *"Look He is coming with the clouds, and every eye will see*
> *Him, even those who pierced him; and all the peoples of the*
> *earth will mourn because of Him. So shall it be! Amen."*
> *Revelation 1:7 NIV*

Every believer knows that Jesus is coming back for us. No one knows
the exact date or time. What we do know is that every second that
goes by brings us closer to His second coming. Revelation 1:7 gives
us insight as to how He will come, "with the clouds." This time "every
eye will see Him." What a dominating presence that will be. Everyone
will "mourn because of Him." Some will mourn because they did not
believe, some because their faith was weak, and some just because
the reality of the cross and the resurrection will be made known to
them. I pray that we will be in the last group. Be ready my dear brothers and sisters. Be on the lookout for His second coming. Expect it
and do not be caught by surprise.

Have a Blessed Day! Follow Him! One Less Day to Go!

God blessed me today, when He:

_____

_____

God used me today when I:

_____

_____

I need to ask God to forgive me today for:

_____

_____

MAY 17

May the peace of our Lord Jesus Christ be with you!

> *"Then Heaven and earth and all that is in them will shout for joy over Babylon, for out of the north destroyers will attack her," declares the Lord."*
> *Jeremiah 51:48 NIV*

Our Lord, His believers, and His children always have the last laugh. The enemy may think they are victorious over God's people. They do not know that when a Christian dies he/she goes home to be with His/her Father. So even in death we are victorious. Death is never final for a Christian but it sure is for a non-believer. Let us be strong in our faith. Let us be patient knowing that the battle is already won and we are just waiting for the victor's shout for joy.

Have a Blessed Day! Follow Him! One Less Day to Go!

God blessed me today, when He:

_____

_____

_____

God used me today when I:

_____

_____

_____

I need to ask God to forgive me today for:

_____

_____

_____

_____

MAY 18

May the peace of our Lord Jesus Christ be with you!

> *"But the eyes of the Lord are on those who fear Him, on those whose hope is in His unfailing love, to deliver them from death and keep them alive in famine."*
> *Psalm 33:18 & 19 NIV*

Our Lord watches over us at all times. His eyes are on us and He sees all. What an assurance of knowing that the Almighty, all-powerful God has His eyes on you and me. His purpose is not to condemn us but to deliver us from death. We who are alive in Jesus cannot die. This deserves a big Amen and Praise the Lord! Thank You Lord for watching over us.

Have a Blessed Day! Follow Him! One Less Day to Go!

God blessed me today, when He:

_____
_____
_____

God used me today when I:

_____
_____
_____

I need to ask God to forgive me today for:

_____
_____
_____

_____

MAY 19

May the peace of our Lord Jesus Christ be with you!

> *"Simon Peter went up, and drew the net to land full of great fishes, an hundred and fifty and three; and for all there were so many, yet was the net not broken."*
> John 21:11

This could have been Simon Peter's last fishing trip. He became a fisher of men after His restoration. Any fishing he did in the ocean was a hobby. His full time job was changed to fisher of men and look how successful he was. His first sermon resulted in about 3000 souls being saved, see Acts 2:41. We may not get the opportunity like Peter, but if we could introduce one sinner to Jesus and he/she repents of their sins and becomes a Christian, we have done well. There are no limits to how many souls can go to Heaven. May we seek out those who need to hear the Gospel and may we be strong and courageous to extend the invitation.

Have a Blessed Day! Follow Him! One Less Day to Go!

God blessed me today, when He:

_____
_____
_____

God used me today when I:

_____
_____
_____

I need to ask God to forgive me today for:

_____
_____
_____
_____

MAY 20

May the peace of our Lord Jesus Christ be with you!

> *"All this is for your benefit, so that the grace that is reaching more and more people may cause thanksgiving to overflow to the glory of God."*
> *2 Corinthians 4:15 NIV*

Everything Jesus did and continues to do is for our benefit (everything). We need to look for the benefit in everything that comes our way, especially while we live on this earth. People find what they look for. If we look for the benefit, we will find it. If we look for the loss we will find it. We will not be disappointed. So let us ask our Father to open our eyes to see the benefits that He provides every day.

Have a Blessed Day! Follow Him! One Less Day to Go!

God blessed me today, when He:

_____
_____
_____

God used me today when I:

_____
_____
_____

I need to ask God to forgive me today for:

_____
_____
_____

_____

MAY 21

May the peace of our Lord Jesus Christ be with you!

> *"May the God who gives endurance and encouragement give you a spirit of unity among yourselves as you follow Christ Jesus, so that with one heart and mouth you may glorify the God and Father of our Lord Jesus Christ."*
> Romans 15: 5 & 6 NIV

Paul's prayer for the Roman Christians is so applicable for us today. We need to be of one heart and voice in these times. May we unite to glorify our Father. Note that God gives endurance and encouragement; He gives a spirit of unity. Are we receiving and accepting these gifts? Let us open our hearts and minds to these gifts from God so we can endure and be encouraged every day. So when you go to church on Sunday; you go to unite with other believers in heart and voice. This is pleasing to the Lord.

Have a Blessed Day! Follow Him! One Less Day to Go!

God blessed me today, when He:

_____

_____

_____

God used me today when I:

_____

_____

_____

I need to ask God to forgive me today for:

_____

_____

_____

MAY 22

May the peace of our Lord Jesus Christ be with you!

> *"I looked for a man among them who will build up the wall and stand before Me in the gap on behalf of the land so I would not have to destroy it, but I found none."*
> Ezekiel 22:30 NIV

Our God could not find a perfect man to save us from His wrath and judgment; yet, He did not give up on us. He sent His only Son, Jesus. It is He who stands in the gap thereby saving us from judgment because He took our place on the cross. Thank you Father for loving us so much that You would send Your Son Jesus to save us. Have you accepted Jesus as your Lord and Savior? Now is as good a time as any.

Have a Blessed Day! Follow Him! One Less Day to Go!

God blessed me today, when He:

_____
_____
_____

God used me today when I:

_____
_____
_____

I need to ask God to forgive me today for:

_____
_____
_____

_____

MAY 23

May the peace of our Lord Jesus Christ be with you!

> *"It was for the sake of the Name that they went out, receiving no help from the pagans. We ought therefore to show hospitality to such men so that we may work together for the truth."*
> *3 John 7&8 NIV*

Our missionaries, pastors and all who serve the Lord (the Name) cannot expect support and help from the unbelievers. We who believe 'ought' to provide support to these men and women who have given up all to serve the Lord. John is telling us that when we support 'such men' we partner with them to spread the Gospel. Support is not limited to money. We 'ought' to pray for them and encourage them. Pray that the Lord will guide you to support who He wants you to support. He will provide.

Have a Blessed Day! Follow Him! One Less Day to Go!

God blessed me today, when He:

_____

_____

_____

God used me today when I:

_____

_____

_____

I need to ask God to forgive me today for:

_____

_____

_____

MAY 24

May the peace of our Lord Jesus Christ be with you!

> *"As the eyes of slaves look to the hand of their master, as the eyes of a maid look to the hand of her mistress, so our eyes look to the Lord our God, till He shows us His mercy."*
> *Psalm 123:2 NIV*

Too many people are looking for mercy and salvation in the wrong place. What's worse are; those who do not believe that they need salvation and mercy. May we who believe always look towards our Father and never look away. Remember what happened to Peter when he looked away from Jesus - he sank in the lake and Jesus still rescued him. So keep your eyes on the Lord! He will show us His mercy.

Have a Blessed Day! Follow Him! One Less Day to Go!

God blessed me today, when He:

_____
_____
_____

God used me today when I:

_____
_____
_____

I need to ask God to forgive me today for:

_____
_____
_____

MAY 25

May the peace of our Lord Jesus Christ be with you!

> *"The voice spoke to him a second time, "Do not call anything*
> *impure that God has made clean.""*
> Acts 10:15 NIV

We are quick to judge and condemn others. We often compare ourselves with others to show how much better we are. However the
Bible is very direct in commanding us that we must not judge or
condemn. We do not know who God has saved or who He has not.
Our responsibility is to make sure we glorify Him in all that we do.
That person who may be a little different than us could be a Spiritual
brother or sister. So let us love our neighbor as ourselves and leave
the judging to The Judge - Our Lord.

Have a Blessed Day! Follow Him! One Less Day to Go!

God blessed me today, when He:

_____

_____

_____

God used me today when I:

_____

_____

_____

I need to ask God to forgive me today for:

_____

_____

_____

_____

MAY 26

May the peace of our Lord Jesus Christ be with you!

> *"And afterward, I will pour out My Spirit on all people. Your sons and daughters will prophesy, your old men will dream dreams, your young men will see visions."*
> *Joel 2:28 NIV*

Our Lord is pouring out His Spirit on all people. We who believe must be aware and listen, both young and old. The only way we will know if other people are full of the Spirit is if we too are full of the Spirit. That's why it is so important for us to study God's word, so we can recognize true messengers from false prophets. Open your hearts and minds to receive the pouring out of The Holy Spirit.

Have a Blessed Day! Follow Him! One Less Day to Go!

God blessed me today, when He:

_____
_____
_____

God used me today when I:

_____
_____
_____

I need to ask God to forgive me today for:

_____
_____
_____

_____

MAY 27

May the peace of our Lord Jesus Christ be with you!

> *"My prayer is not for them alone. I pray also for those who will believe in Me through their message, that all of them may be one, Father, just as You are in Me and I am in You. May they also be in us so that the world May believe that You have sent Me."* John 17: 20 & 21 NIV

This is part of the prayer of our Lord Jesus Christ on the night He was arrested to be crucified. He is about to face the greatest trial of anyone; and who is He praying for? -You and me. Our Lord wants us to be like Him. He wants us to be one in Spirit just like He and His Father. So how do we respond? We fall down on our knees in awe and say thank You Jesus. When we accept Him and He lives in us, then everyone we come into contact with will see Him and know that we are like Him. May our thoughts, speech and actions be a reflection of Jesus Christ!

Have a Blessed Day! Follow Him! One Less Day to Go!

God blessed me today, when He:

_____

_____

_____

God used me today when I:

_____

_____

_____

I need to ask God to forgive me today for:

_____

_____

_____

MAY 28

May the peace of our Lord Jesus Christ be with you!

> *"He will not let your foot slip -- He who watches over you will*
> *not slumber."*
> *Psalm 121: 3 NIV*

Our Heavenly Father will not allow us to stumble if we look to Him.
We stumble when we seek guidance from other sources and when
we act without consulting Him. Our Lord is always looking over us.
May we remember this in good times and bad times. He is there
awake and alert. All we need to do is look to Him.

Have a Blessed Day! Follow Him! One Less Day to Go!

God blessed me today, when He:

_____

_____

_____

God used me today when I:

_____

_____

_____

I need to ask God to forgive me today for:

_____

_____

_____

MAY 29

May the peace of our Lord Jesus Christ be with you!

> *"Once, having been asked by the Pharisees when the king-dom of God would come, Jesus replied, "The kingdom of God does not come visibly; nor will people say, 'Here is it, or there is it, because the kingdom of God is within you.""*
> *Luke 17:20 & 21 NIV*

The kingdom of God is a place of love, peace, sharing, kindness, and worshipping God. Do our lives reflect these qualities? Jesus clearly says that the kingdom of God is within us and what's within us is what will come out of us. May our lives be an example of the kingdom of God.

Have a Blessed Day! Follow Him! One Less Day to Go!

God blessed me today, when He:

_____
_____
_____

God used me today when I:

_____
_____
_____

I need to ask God to forgive me today for:

_____
_____
_____

MAY 30

May the peace of our Lord Jesus Christ be with you!

> *"Know that the Lord is God. It is He who made us, and we are*
> *His; we are His people; the sheep of His pasture."*
> Psalm 100:3 NIV

To know is to believe - the Lord is God. He made us and He made us
in His image. It is better to be a sheep in God's pasture than a king in
the devil's city. Our shepherd will lay His life down for us. His command to Peter was - 'Feed My sheep.' He is always looking out for us.
May we always remember that we worship a God who is Lord!

Have a Blessed Day! Follow Him! One Less Day to Go!

God blessed me today, when He:

_____

_____

_____

God used me today when I:

_____

_____

_____

I need to ask God to forgive me today for:

_____

_____

_____

MAY 31

May the peace of our Lord Jesus Christ be with you!

> *"Yes, and I ask you, loyal yoke fellow, help those women who have contended at my side in the cause of the gospel, along with Clement and the rest of my fellow workers, whose names are in the book of life."*
> *Philippians 4:3 NIV*

This verse offers so much for us today. Paul uses some critical words - 'loyal; fellow workers and yoke fellow.' Loyal and fellow workers are common but 'yoke fellow.' What's a 'yoke fellow?' We have friends who only come around when there is a party or some fun thing happening. A 'yoke fellow' is the one you see or hear from when things are going bad. The one who visits in the hospital. The one who sticks with you when everyone else abandons you. That's a yoke fellow. We all need a yoke fellow. Jesus will always be our yoke fellow. Be a yoke fellow to someone today. That's one way to get your name into the 'book of life.'

Have a Blessed Day! Follow Him! One Less Day to Go!

God blessed me today, when He:

_____

_____

_____

God used me today when I:

_____

_____

_____

I need to ask God to forgive me today for:

_____

_____

_____

JUNE 1

May the peace of our Lord Jesus Christ be with you!

> "The Lord redeems His servants; no one who takes refuge in
> Him will be condemned."
> Psalm 34:22 NIV

We cannot serve two masters. We either serve the Lord or the devil.
Servants of the devil end up in disappointment and hell. Servants of
the Lord end up in Heaven. Man may condemn us and that's ok because it is temporary. If a person is condemned by God, that's permanent. We cannot redeem ourselves. We cannot defend ourselves. We
need the grace of our Lord to redeem us and save us from condemnation. So let us seek His face and live with Him. He is our shield.

Have a Blessed Day! Follow Him! One Less Day to Go!

God blessed me today, when He:

_____
_____
_____

God used me today when I:

_____
_____
_____

I need to ask God to forgive me today for:

_____
_____
_____

_____

JUNE 2

May the peace of our Lord Jesus Christ be with you!

> When Jesus spoke again to the people; He said, "I am the light
> of the world. Whoever follows Me will never walk in darkness,
> but will have the light of life."
> John 8:12 NIV

We must remember that we who believe and follow Jesus walk in the light. We live in a world full of darkness. When there is more darkness, the need for light is greater. One candle can provide light for many. We have access to the brightest light that shines. May our prayer be for the light of Jesus Christ to shine brightly through us so many will come to walk in His light and have everlasting life. Is His light shining brightly through you? Brothers and sisters, do not allow the cares of this world to cover our light.

Have a Blessed Day! Follow Him! One Less Day to Go!

God blessed me today, when He:

_____
_____
_____

God used me today when I:

_____
_____
_____

I need to ask God to forgive me today for:

_____
_____
_____

JUNE 3

May the peace of our Lord Jesus Christ be with you!

> *"Salt is good, but if it loses its saltiness, how can it be made*
> *salty again? It is fit neither for the soil nor for the manure pile;*
> *it is thrown out."*
> *Luke 14:34 & 35 NIV*

This is a warning from Jesus to those who choose to serve other Gods. Once we accept Jesus as lord and Savior we also choose to follow His way. Some slip and turn back to their old selves and that's when they begin to lose their "saltiness," - their faith and fire for Jesus. Complacency is a sure sign of losing your "saltiness." Let us pray that we will be strong in our faith and beliefs, so that we will remain in His Grace and not be thrown out.

Have a Blessed Day! Follow Him! One Less Day to Go!

God blessed me today, when He:

_____

_____

_____

God used me today when I:

_____

_____

_____

I need to ask God to forgive me today for:

_____

_____

_____

_____

JUNE 4

May the peace of our Lord Jesus Christ be with you!

> *"Praise the Lord. I will extol the Lord with all my heart in the council of the upright and in the assembly."*
> *Psalm 111:1 NIV*

Are you an active worshipper or passive? The psalmist encourages us to worship and praise the Lord with all our hearts everywhere we go. May we praise the Lord and lift Him up. May we assemble in numbers to worship and praise Him. I pray that when He comes back, He will find us praising and worshipping Him.

Have a Blessed Day! Follow Him! One Less Day to Go!

God blessed me today, when He:

_____

_____

_____

God used me today when I:

_____

_____

_____

I need to ask God to forgive me today for:

_____

_____

_____

JUNE 5

May the peace of our Lord Jesus Christ be with you!

> *"O my Strength, I watch for You; You, O God, are my fortress."*
> *Psalm 59:9 NIV*

Our strength comes from the Lord. When we feel weak, let us remember that our Father is strong and He protects us from all evil. To "watch for You" means to wait. Let us be patient and watch how the Lord protects us and fights our battles. Victory is certain when we wait on the Lord.

Have a Blessed Day! Follow Him! One Less Day to Go!

God blessed me today, when He:

_____

_____

_____

God used me today when I:

_____

_____

_____

I need to ask God to forgive me today for:

_____

_____

_____

JUNE 6

May the peace of our Lord Jesus Christ be with you!

> "Then Peter said, "Silver or gold, I do not have, but what I have,
> I give you. In the name of Jesus Christ of Nazareth, walk.""
> Acts 3:6 NIV

This man who Peter is talking to was crippled. Peter, in the name of Jesus, healed him. Let us focus on Peter's opening statement: "Silver or gold, I do not have, but what I have, I give you." We cannot give what we do not have. But we have the most precious gift we can give to anyone, a way to salvation. We who believe have a relationship with Jesus that we can share with others. In fact our Lord expects us to share Him with others. May we be alert to the one who needs to hear the Gospel message and may we be faithful to share. Introduce someone to Jesus today.

Have a Blessed Day! Follow Him! One Less Day to Go!

God blessed me today, when He:

_____
_____
_____

God used me today when I:

_____
_____
_____

I need to ask God to forgive me today for:

_____
_____
_____
_____

JUNE 7

May the peace of our Lord Jesus Christ be with you!

> *"I love You, O Lord, my strength. The Lord is my rock, my fortress
> and my deliverer: my God is my rock, in whom I take refuge.
> He is my shield and the horn of my salvation, my stronghold."*
> *Psalm 18: 1 & 2 NIV*

What more do we need? I would suggest we print this verse and have it visible and close to us as a constant reminder. We belong to the God who is our rock when storms hit us. His rock will stand firm. He is our fortress to protect us from the devil and his evil ways. He is our deliverer to rescue us when we do succumb to temptation. May we learn to trust Him more for He is our only hope of salvation. When we stand with Him we are safe where no harm can come to us. Try committing this verse to memory and make it a daily prayer. We need our God.

Have a Blessed Day! Follow Him! One Less Day to Go!

God blessed me today, when He:

_____

_____

_____

God used me today when I:

_____

_____

_____

I need to ask God to forgive me today for:

_____

_____

_____

JUNE 8

May the peace of our Lord Jesus Christ be with you!

> *"From the throne came flashes of lightning, rumblings and peals of thunder. Before the throne seven lamps were blazing. These are the seven spirits of God."*
> *Revelation 4:5 NIV*

Heaven is for real! This is not a description of special effects. This is John's witness of what he saw. God is showing us a glimpse of what Heaven is like through the eyes of John. Read Revelation Chapter 4 and note the details. Heaven is for real and it's no ordinary place. It is a unique and spectacular place. There is a mansion waiting for those who believe and accept Jesus as Lord and Savior.

Have a Blessed Day! Follow Him! One Less Day to Go!

God blessed me today, when He:

_____
_____
_____

God used me today when I:

_____
_____
_____

I need to ask God to forgive me today for:

_____
_____
_____

JUNE 9

May the peace of our Lord Jesus Christ be with you!

> *"The light shines in the darkness, but the darkness has not understood it."*
> *John 1:5 NIV*

This verse was written approximately 2000 years ago after the death and resurrection of Jesus Christ. Take note of the tense. It's written in present tense, meaning the Light (Jesus) is still shining and there are many who still do not understand. Understanding comes from faith and trust in Jesus. It comes from total surrender to Him and still there will be things we do not fully understand, but accept in faith. One day we will understand clearly. I pray that you and I will seek to understand Him.

Have a Blessed Day! Follow Him! One Less Day to Go!

God blessed me today, when He:

_____

_____

_____

God used me today when I:

_____

_____

_____

I need to ask God to forgive me today for:

_____

_____

_____

_____

JUNE 10

May the peace of our Lord Jesus Christ be with you!

> *"Therefore He is able to save completely those who come to God through Him, because He always lives to intercede for them."*
> *Hebrews 7:25 NIV*

Our Lord never does anything halfway. He completely saves us. He is not a God who comes and goes but a God who "always lives to intercede for us." What a humbling honor and privilege that the Almighty Jesus will intercede for you and me. We who believe are assured of our salvation because Jesus is the one who intercedes for us. He has never lost a case. Thank You Jesus for standing between us and the judgment of God.

Have a Blessed day! Follow Him! One Less Day to Go!

God blessed me today, when He:

_____
_____
_____

God used me today when I:

_____
_____
_____

I need to ask God to forgive me today for:

_____
_____
_____

_____

JUNE 11

May the peace of our Lord Jesus Christ be with you!

> *"Consequently, faith comes from hearing the message, and the message is heard through the word of Christ."*
> *Romans 10:17 NIV*

The message is the word of Christ. Every one of us heard the message from someone else (a pastor, parent, friend etc.). There are many more people who need to hear the message. We who have heard the message, and believe, must now become messengers. Share the message with someone today.

Have a Blessed Day! Follow Him! One Less Day to Go!

God blessed me today, when He:

_____

_____

_____

God used me today when I:

_____

_____

_____

I need to ask God to forgive me today for:

_____

_____

_____

JUNE 12

May the peace of our Lord Jesus Christ be with you!

> *"So will it be with the resurrection of the dead. The body that is sown is perishable; it is sown in dishonor, it is raised in glory; it is sown in weakness, it is raised in power; it is sown a natural body, it is raised a spiritual body."*
> 1 Corinthians 15:42 - 44

Paul is talking about our bodies, yours and mine. This is what we have to look forward to: glory, power, and a spiritual body. This is why Christians die full of hope and faith. We know death is not final but a transition to a place that's so much better than what we have here. Meanwhile we live full lives serving and praising our Holy Father!

Have a Blessed Day! Follow Him! One Less Day to Go!

God blessed me today, when He:

_____
_____
_____

God used me today when I:

_____
_____
_____

I need to ask God to forgive me today for:

_____
_____
_____

_____

JUNE 13

May the peace of our Lord Jesus Christ be with you!

> *"Let them give thanks to the Lord for His unfailing love, and His wonderful deeds for men, for He satisfies the thirsty and fills the hungry with good things."*
> *Psalm 107: 8 & 9 NIV*

We who believe, are children of the Heavenly Father. Every day is Father's day for Him. His love for us is unfailing and when He blesses His children; its wonderful not just ordinary. We need to give our Heavenly Father thanks more often for all that He does for us. May we feed on His word and never go hungry or thirsty.

Have a Blessed Day! Follow Him! One Less Day to Go!

God blessed me today, when He:

_____
_____
_____

God used me today when I:

_____
_____
_____

I need to ask God to forgive me today for:

_____
_____
_____

JUNE 14

May the peace of our Lord Jesus Christ be with you!

> *"Others, like seed sown on good soil, hear the word, accept it, and produce a crop - thirty, sixty or even a hundred times what was sown."*
> *Mark 4:20 NIV*

Read Mark 4 verses 1 to 20. This is a well-known parable. Many make the excuse that they were the seed that fell among thorns or on rocky ground. Jesus' explanation of the parable contradicts that excuse. The word "like" is a key word in His explanation to not just the disciples, but you and me. We choose to accept the word or not to accept. We will know whether we accept the word by the way we live our lives. How many souls are we touching in a positive, constructive way? How many souls are we introducing to Jesus? Remember God does not use the same measuring system as man. The question we need to ask ourselves is: are we being the best that God designed us to be?

Have a Blessed Day! Follow Him! One Less Day to Go!

God blessed me today, when He:

_____
_____
_____

God used me today when I:

_____
_____
_____

I need to ask God to forgive me today for:

_____
_____
_____

JUNE 15

May the peace of our Lord Jesus Christ be with you!

> "Salt is good, but if it loses its saltiness, how can you make
> it salty again? Have salt in yourselves, and be at peace with
> each other."
> Mark 9:50 NIV

Salt can be anything. It can be love, obedience, patience, tolerance, or faith. When we invite the Holy Spirit to come and dwell inside of us, it is our responsibility to maintain a strong and steady relationship with Him. We cannot be Christ-like on some days and not on other days. We cannot be Christ-like for some people and evil for others. We must always be like Him and live in peace with one another. When people come into contact with you or do business with you do they see the Holy Spirit, the salt, in you? God help us to be consistent in our walk.

Have a Blessed Day! Follow Him! One Less Day to Go!

God blessed me today, when He:

_____

_____

_____

God used me today when I:

_____

_____

_____

I need to ask God to forgive me today for:

_____

_____

_____

_____

JUNE 16

May the peace of our Lord Jesus Christ be with you!

> *"Then I will teach transgressors Your ways, and sinners will turn back to You."*
> Psalm 51:13 NIV

Our role as teachers of the Gospel is not to make people feel worse than they already feel or to make them feel less than us. Our purpose is to bring them back into God's adopted family. When we lead one sinner back to Jesus there is rejoicing in Heaven. Let's start with ourselves. Remember what the father did when the Prodigal son returned home, he made a feast. That's what our Heavenly Father will do when we turn back to Him. There are many people who need to learn about the saving Grace of Jesus Christ. They can only learn it from someone who knows about it and have experienced it and owns it.

Have a Blessed Day! Follow Him! One Less Day to Go!

God blessed me today, when He:

_____
_____
_____

God used me today when I:

_____
_____
_____

I need to ask God to forgive me today for:

_____
_____
_____
_____

JUNE 17

May the peace of our Lord Jesus Christ be with you!

> *"I rejoiced with those who said to me, "Let us go to the house*
> *of the Lord.""*
> Psalm 122:1 NIV

May we join with those who worship in the house of the Lord and not be distracted by the devil. He will try to influence us with so many excuses for not going to church. The psalmist David encourages us to go and worship in God's house. May we learn to go with joy and not out of a sense of duty.

Have a Blessed Day! Follow Him! One Less Day to Go!

God blessed me today, when He:

_____

_____

_____

God used me today when I:

_____

_____

_____

I need to ask God to forgive me today for:

_____

_____

_____

JUNE 18

May the peace of our Lord Jesus Christ be with you!

> *"Bless those who persecute you; bless and do not curse."*
> *Romans 12:14 NIV*

We can only bless those who persecute us, and not curse, if we are filled with the Holy Spirit. Christians have been persecuted from the beginning. Persecution is a sort of confirmation that you are Christian. The times ahead will be filled with more persecution of Christians. We should expect it because we are different. The way we respond to persecution is also different. We bless those who persecute us with the power of the Grace of our Father.

Have a Blessed Day! Follow Him! One Less Day to Go!

God blessed me today, when He:

_____
_____
_____

God used me today when I:

_____
_____
_____

I need to ask God to forgive me today for:

_____
_____
_____

JUNE 19

May the peace of our Lord Jesus Christ be with you!

> *"Who shall separate us from the love of Christ? Shall trouble*
> *or hardship or persecution or famine or nakedness or danger*
> *or sword?"*
> *Romans 8:35 NIV*

The answer is nothing and no one other than ourselves. Our Lord has promised that He will never leave us nor forsake us. When we feel lonely, let us remember He is right there beside us. His love is all we really need. It is God's love for us and in us that equips us to love others. Remember nothing can separate us from His love.

Have a Blessed Day! Follow Him! One Less Day to Go!

God blessed me today, when He:

_____

_____

_____

God used me today when I:

_____

_____

_____

I need to ask God to forgive me today for:

_____

_____

_____

JUNE 20

May the peace of our Lord Jesus Christ be with you!

> "Whoever does not love does not know God, because God
> is love."
> 1 John 4:8 NIV

The love that John refers to here is the true, genuine, unconditional love of our Father in Heaven. This is not a love that comes and goes. It is a love that's everlasting. When we begin to experience this love from our Father then we can also love like Him. Father thank You for Your love for us and may we learn to love like You.

Have a Blessed Day! Follow Him! One Less Day to Go!

God blessed me today, when He:

_____
_____
_____

God used me today when I:

_____
_____
_____

I need to ask God to forgive me today for:

_____
_____
_____

JUNE 21

May the peace of our Lord Jesus Christ be with us!

> "Do not be afraid of them, for I am with you and will rescue
> you," declares the Lord."
> Jeremiah 1:8 NIV

Our Lord is with us and He will rescue us from all evil. May we walk
without fear of the enemy because we have the power of the Holy
Spirit with us. There is no one or thing more powerful than our Father.
Place whatever is haunting you or causing you to be afraid at God's
feet and He will take care of it. That's His promise. Our Lord keeps
every promise He makes.

Have a Blessed Day! Follow Him! One Less Day to Go!

God blessed me today, when He:

_____

_____

_____

God used me today when I:

_____

_____

_____

I need to ask God to forgive me today for:

_____

_____

_____

JUNE 22

May the peace of our Lord Jesus Christ be with you!

> *"He guides the humble in what is right and teaches them His way."*
> *Psalm 25:9 NIV*

Our Lord is our guide and teacher. He guides us in the right way. It is our responsibility to follow His guidance. May we continue to walk in the path that He guides us and not stray away. He teaches us his way. It is our choice to learn and practice His way. Our Lord will protect us as long as we walk in His way. We will be hurt when we choose other paths to walk. Choose wisely by dear brothers and sisters. His way is the only way!

Have a Blessed Day! Follow Him! One Less Day to Go!

God blessed me today, when He:

_____
_____
_____

God used me today when I:

_____
_____
_____

I need to ask God to forgive me today for:

_____
_____
_____

_____

JUNE 23

May the peace of our Lord Jesus Christ be with you!

> *"My command is this: Love each other as I have loved you."*
> *John 15:12 NIV*

This is not a wish or a suggestion. It's a direct command from our Lord and Savior. If you are not sure about how Jesus loves us read John 15: 9 - 17 and John 3:16. When we are tempted to hate someone, let us remember our Lord's command. If He can love me then I can love anyone. I can love anyone because of Him that is in me. God's love for us is an everyday love. His love is not just for a season or special occasion. Thank You Lord for loving us so much.

Have a Blessed Day! Follow Him! One Less Day to Go!

God blessed me today, when He:

_____
_____
_____

God used me today when I:

_____
_____
_____

I need to ask God to forgive me today for:

_____
_____
_____

JUNE 24

May the peace of our Lord Jesus Christ be with you!

> "It is Mine to avenge; I will repay. In due time their foot will slip; their day of disaster is near and their doom rushes upon them."
> Deuteronomy 32:35 NIV

The murder of Christians by terrorists should impact all Christians because history has a way of repeating itself. The fallen are our brothers in Christ. We know that they are resting with our Father right now. Many will be tempted to seek vengeance, but that's God's work. Vengeance is mine says the Lord. Let us pray for peace and comfort for the surviving families and leave vengeance up to the Lord. His judgment is sure and on time.

Have a Blessed Day! Follow Him! One Less Day to Go!

God blessed me today, when He:

_____

_____

_____

God used me today when I:

_____

_____

_____

I need to ask God to forgive me today for:

_____

_____

_____

_____

JUNE 25

May the peace of our Lord Jesus Christ be with you!

"Show the wonder of Your great love, You who save by Your right hand those who take refuge in You from their foes."
Psalm 17:7 NIV

Many Christian brothers and sisters are being prosecuted every day in all parts of the world - some directly and some indirectly. Many have to worship in private secret places. We who are fortunate to be able to worship and practice our faith openly must always remember those who can't; in our daily prayers. Our Lord is faithful to protect His children from the enemy. Pray that those who are being prosecuted will continue to put their trust in God.

Have a Blessed Day! Follow Him! One Less Day to Go!

God blessed me today, when He:

_____
_____
_____

God used me today when I:

_____
_____
_____

I need to ask God to forgive me today for:

_____
_____
_____

_____

JUNE 26

May the peace of our Lord Jesus Christ be with you!

"May the glory of the Lord endure forever; may the Lord rejoice in His works."
Psalm 104:31 NIV

How can we contribute to God's glory? It is good to wish and pray that His glory endures forever, but we can do so much more to ensure that His glory endures forever. He delights in our good works. We are His works. He created us to glorify Him. So let us look for opportunities to serve Him. Let us look for His Divine intervention and victory in every situation. May our thoughts, words and actions glorify our Lord.

Have a Blessed Day! Follow Him! One Less Day to Go!

God blessed me today, when He:

_____
_____
_____

God used me today when I:

_____
_____
_____

I need to ask God to forgive me today for:

_____
_____
_____

_____

JUNE 27

May the peace of our Lord Jesus Christ be with you!

> "For the Scripture says to Pharaoh: "I raised you up for this very purpose, that I might display My power in you and that My name might be proclaimed in all the earth.""
> Romans 9:17 NIV

It looks like a lot of bad people are getting away with evil today. But we must be strong in our faith and trust that God knows what He is doing. He is in control and His day will come when all these evil people will suffer the consequences of their actions against God's children. Pharaoh is just one example of God's power and justice. Our Lord is more powerful than any force or organization.

Have a Blessed Day! Follow Him! One Less Day to Go!

God blessed me today, when He:

_____

_____

_____

God used me today when I:

_____

_____

_____

I need to ask God to forgive me today for:

_____

_____

_____

JUNE 28

May the peace of our Lord Jesus Christ be with you!

> *"Neither has Herod for he sent him back to us; as you can see, He has done nothing wrong to deserve death."*
> *Luke 23:15 NIV*

Both Herod and Pilate could not find any evidence that Jesus had done any wrong deserving of death. They were both right. It is you and I who deserve the punishment of death. Jesus took our place and died for us. We should say, 'Thank You Jesus for dying on the cross for my sins', every day of our lives here on Earth. May we never forget what our Savior did on the cross for us. That's the foundation of our faith and belief. He died and rose from the grave. Now we live because He died. Thank You Lord!

Have a Blessed Day! Follow Him! One Less Day to Go!

God blessed me today, when He:

_____

_____

_____

God used me today when I:

_____

_____

_____

I need to ask God to forgive me today for:

_____

_____

_____

JUNE 29

May the peace of our Lord Jesus Christ be with you!

> *"So neither he who plants nor he who waters is anything, but only God who makes things grow."*
> *1 Corinthians 3:7 NIV*

Nothing good is ever accomplished without the Grace of God. That's why we must always consult with our Lord before doing anything. We tend to get so busy doing; that we forget we have a source of power and wisdom that is better than any. Let us be more intentional about seeking God's wisdom before doing anything and when we accomplish greatness let us give Him the glory. We are nothing without God; and so much with Him.

Have a Blessed Day! Follow Him! One Less Day to Go!

God blessed me today, when He:

_____
_____
_____

God used me today when I:

_____
_____
_____

I need to ask God to forgive me today for:

_____
_____
_____

_____

JUNE 30

May the peace of our Lord Jesus Christ be with you!

> *"But I trust in You, O Lord; I say, "You are my God," My times are in Your hands; deliver me from my enemies and from those who pursue me."*
> *Psalm 31:14 & 15 NIV*

Our Lord is in full control of all that's going on in our lives. When we learn to totally trust Him we know that He will deliver us from any evil that may come our way. Let us not limit our enemies to other people. Anything that separates us from the presence of our Heavenly Father is an enemy. May we remain in His hands and not drift away.

Have a Blessed Day! Follow Him! One Less Day to Go!

God blessed me today, when He:

_____
_____
_____

God used me today when I:

_____
_____
_____

I need to ask God to forgive me today for:

_____
_____
_____

_____

JULY 1

May the peace of our Lord Jesus Christ be with you!

> *"Then the word of the Lord came to me; "O house of Israel,
> can I not do with you as this potter does?" declares the Lord.
> "Like clay in the hand of the potter, so are you in my hand, O
> house of Israel.""*

Jeremiah 18: 5 & 6 NIV

We too are 'like clay in the hand of the potter.' God created us; we did not create Him. We belong to Him and He can do anything He wants with us and all of His creation. He alone is Almighty. So why do we resist? Why do we want to do our own thing? It is best for us to let Him have His way with us. He knows best. He is our Father. He will shape us into the finest person, if we let Him have His way.

Have a Blessed Day! Follow Him! One Less Day to Go!

God blessed me today, when He:

_____
_____
_____

God used me today when I:

_____
_____
_____

I need to ask God to forgive me today for:

_____
_____
_____
_____

JULY 2

May the peace of our Lord Jesus Christ be with you!

> *"As it is written in the book of the words of Isaiah the prophet: 'A voice of one calling in the desert, 'Prepare the way for the Lord, make straight paths for Him. Every valley shall be filled in, every mountain and hill made low. The crooked roads shall become straight, the rough ways smooth. And all mankind shall see God's salvation.'"*
> *Luke 3:4-6 NIV*

John the Baptist's message is just as relevant and urgent today as it was when he first delivered it. May we listen to his message today as we are so much closer to the second coming. Let us prepare the way for Jesus to enter into our hearts. Let us remove every barrier and distraction right now; because no one knows the hour when He will come. Lord, help us to focus on you and ignore the distractions of this world. May we be ready when you come again.

Have a Blessed Day! Follow Him! One Less Day to Go!

God blessed me today, when He:

_____

_____

_____

God used me today when I:

_____

_____

_____

I need to ask God to forgive me today for:

_____

_____

_____

JULY 3

May the peace of our Lord Jesus Christ be with you!

> *"You belong to your father, the devil, and you want to carry out your father's desire. He was a murderer from the beginning, not holding to the truth, for there is no truth in him. When he lies, he speaks his native language, for he is a liar and father of lies."*
> *John 8:44 NIV*

Jesus clearly describes the character of the devil for us. It is advantageous to be aware of the enemy. We must be able to recognize the devil when he comes to tempt us. Anything that is not of Jesus is a lie. That's why we need to know the Word of the Lord. If we do not know the truth how can we recognize the lies. Brothers and sisters, study the Word of the Lord so you will be able to recognize the lies. When you are not sure, ask God to let you know before taking action.

Have a Blessed Day! Follow Him! One Less Day to Go!

God blessed me today, when He:

_____

_____

_____

God used me today when I:

_____

_____

_____

I need to ask God to forgive me today for:

_____

_____

_____

_____

JULY 4

May the peace of our Lord Jesus Christ be with you!

> *"The Lord delights in the way of the man whose steps He has made firm; though he stumble, he will not fall, for the Lord upholds him with His hand."*
> *Psalm 37:23 & 24 NIV*

When we walk in the way of the Lord; He is pleased, Amen. Let us not fool ourselves into thinking that we can obey Him on our own. It is He who strengthens us to obey Him. He is our shepherd and we are His sheep. That's why He will not allow those who accept Him as Lord and Savior to fall. We know when we stumble. Let us thank Him for holding us up and preventing us from falling. The devil wants to pull us down. Our Father wants to lift us up.

Have a Blessed Day! Follow Him! One More day to Go!

God blessed me today, when He:

_____

_____

_____

God used me today when I:

_____

_____

_____

I need to ask God to forgive me today for:

_____

_____

_____

_____

JULY 5

May the peace of our Lord Jesus Christ be with you!

> *"Everyone must submit himself to the governing authorities, for there is no authority except that which God has established. The authorities that exist have been established by God."*
> *Romans 13:1 NIV*

This could be a very hard and challenging verse to obey. What about the tyrants, war mongers, selfish, etc. who are in authority? Should we submit to them? Look at all the bad leaders in History. God took care of them. Everyone who abuses the power that he or she receives from God will suffer God's judgement and wrath. Let God have His way. He is the ultimate judge. May we learn to trust Him fully and obey His word. Pray for His grace to accept those He places in authority over us. When we submit; we submit to God. This is what faith is all about.

Have a Blessed Day! Follow Him! One Less Day to Go!

God blessed me today, when He:

_____
_____
_____

God used me today when I:

_____
_____
_____

I need to ask God to forgive me today for:

_____
_____
_____
_____

JULY 6

May the peace of our Lord Jesus Christ be with you!

> 'To him who overcomes, I will give the right to eat from the tree of life, which is in the paradise of God.'
> Revelation 2:8 NIV

Jesus challenges us to 'overcome' evil. Our reward will be 'the right to eat from the tree of life, which is in the paradise of God.' He told Adam and Eve not to eat of the 'tree of life'. See Genesis 2: 16 & 17. When we overcome, we get to eat of the tree of life. The irony of this is that Jesus Himself helps us to overcome evil. If we are intentional about overcoming evil, we will be more successful. We need to learn to recognize the evil and decide that submitting is not an option. If more married couples will decide that divorce is not an option, we will have more happy marriages. May we seek the help of Jesus in overcoming evil and reap the reward of eating from the tree of life.

Have a Blessed Day! Follow Him! One Less Day to Go!

God blessed me today, when He:

_____
_____
_____

God used me today when I:

_____
_____
_____

I need to ask God to forgive me today for:

_____
_____
_____

JULY 7

May the peace of our Lord Jesus Christ be with you!

> "Simon answered, "Master, we've worked hard all night and haven't caught anything. *But because You say so* I will let down the nets."
> Luke 5:5 NIV

Simon Peter was the professional fisherman. He knew the waters. As far as he was concerned, Jesus was a 'Master' - a great teacher, but no fisherman. 'But because You say so, I will let down the nets.' When the Lord tells us to do something, do we do it like Peter, just because He says so; or do we negotiate with God? Strong faith and trust result in complete and immediate obedience to the Lord. Read the results of Peter's obedience in verses 6 and 7. May we learn to obey our Father, 'because He says so.'

Have a Blessed Day! Follow Him! One Less Day to Go!

God blessed me today, when He:

_____

_____

_____

God used me today when I:

_____

_____

_____

I need to ask God to forgive me today for:

_____

_____

_____

_____

JULY 8

May the peace of our Lord Jesus Christ be with you!

> *"'and receive from Him anything we ask, because we obey His commands and do what pleases Him. And this is His command: to believe in the name of His Son, Jesus Christ, and to love one another as He commanded us.' "*
> *1 John 3:22 & 23 NIV*

Christianity is the simplest religion. All we have to do to please our God (the one and only God) is to believe in Jesus Christ and love one another. We are the ones who tend to complicate matters. Let's be obedient by sticking to His commands and not add any of our own. When we believe in Jesus Christ we will only ask for things that please and glorify Him. Ask and believe that He will provide. Remember we are His children.

Have a Blessed Day! Follow Him! One Less Day to Go!

God blessed me today, when He:

_____

_____

_____

God used me today when I:

_____

_____

_____

I need to ask God to forgive me today for:

_____

_____

_____

JULY 9

May the peace of our Lord Jesus Christ be with you!

> 'We tell you the good news: What God has promised our fathers He has fulfilled for us, their children, by raising up Jesus. As it is written in the second Psalm; "You are My Son; today I have become your Father."'
> Acts 13:32 & 33 NIV

'The good news that Paul shared with the people of his time is still 'good news today. Are you feeling down, depressed about all the bad news going around? Don't be; remember we are God's children and He is our Father. Everything else is trivial compared to this fact. So rejoice my brothers and sisters. We are children of The Almighty God. That's what's most important and permanent.

Have a Blessed Day! Follow Him! One Less Day to Go!

God blessed me today, when He:

_____
_____
_____

God used me today when I:

_____
_____
_____

I need to ask God to forgive me today for:

_____
_____
_____
_____
_____

JULY 10

May the peace of our Lord Jesus Christ be with you!

> *"Before the mountains were born or You brought forth the earth and the world, from everlasting to everlasting You are God."*
> *Psalm 90:2 NIV*

Moses acknowledges the everlasting existence of our Lord. It is good for us to pause ever so often to acknowledge and recognize our Lord Almighty. The circumstances of this world could and do distract us from adoring and worshipping our Lord. Let us make it a daily habit to look up and praise our Heavenly Father. If we are constantly aware of His presence and greatness, we will have more peace and joy in this world.

Have a Blessed Day! Follow Him! One Less Day to Go!

God blessed me today, when He:

_____

_____

_____

God used me today when I:

_____

_____

_____

I need to ask God to forgive me today for:

_____

_____

_____

_____

JULY 11

May the peace of our Lord Jesus Christ be with you!

> 'But He said to me, "My grace is sufficient for you, for my power is made perfect in weakness." Therefore I will boast all the more gladly about my weaknesses, so that Christ's power may rest on me.'
> 2 Corinthians 12:9 NIV

People, including some Christians, who think they are strong do not believe they need help or protection. They are self-sufficient. They think they can protect themselves from anything. It is we who know we are weak; who need a Savior and a protector - Jesus. This is a verse we should all keep close. It's a good verse to commit to memory and when the next trial or temptation comes at us we can say - His Grace is sufficient for me. If we have Jesus, we do not need anything else. The best part is that His Grace is freely given to those who will receive it.

Have a Blessed Day! Follow Him! One Less Day to Go!

God blessed me today, when He:

_____
_____
_____

God used me today when I:

_____
_____
_____

I need to ask God to forgive me today for:

_____
_____
_____

JULY 12

May the peace our Lord Jesus Christ be with you!

> *"Therefore, my dear friends, as you have always obeyed -- not only in my presence, but now much more in my absence -- continue to work out your salvation with fear and trembling, for it is God who works in you to will and to act according to His purpose."*
> *Philippians 2:12 & 13 NIV*

It could be easy to misinterpret this verse regarding 'works' and faith. But verse 13 clears up the debate. When we accept Jesus as Lord and Savior we are saved. That's only one of the reasons He came - to save us. The next reason is to have a relationship with us - to dwell inside of us. Many Christians have accepted His saving grace but have not yet opened their hearts to let Him in. When we take that step, then it is Jesus Christ who inspires us to please and glorify Him with everything we think, say and do. He is in our presence all the time.

Have a Blessed Day! Follow Him! One Less Day to Go!

God blessed me today, when He:

_____
_____
_____

God used me today when I:

_____
_____
_____

I need to ask God to forgive me today for:

_____
_____
_____

JULY 13

May the peace of our Lord Jesus Christ be with you! Sin is NOT our master; Jesus is!!!

> *"Whatever you do, work at it with all your heart, as working for the Lord, not for men, since you know that you will receive an inheritance from the Lord as a reward. It is the Lord Christ you are serving."*
> *Colossians 3:23 & 24 NIV*

Christians do not work. They serve. Our work is all for the glory of our Father. That's why we must always give all we can and never hold back. Our CEO is Jesus Christ Himself. Any reward we receive in this world is nothing compared to the reward waiting for us in Heaven. My prayer for you and me is that when we get to Heaven, our Father will say - 'Well done my child!' May we always remember these 2 verses and commit to do our best at all times.

Have a Blessed Day! Follow Him! One Less Day to Go!

God blessed me today, when He:

_____
_____
_____

God used me today when I:

_____
_____
_____

I need to ask God to forgive me today for:

_____
_____
_____

JULY 14

May the peace of our Lord Jesus Christ be with you!

"You will seek Me and find Me when you seek Me with all your heart."
Jeremiah 29:13 NIV

God is everywhere and yet many cannot find Him. They cannot find Him because they do not intentionally seek Him with all their heart. Our Father knows our hearts. He wants us to find Him but He also wants us to be earnest and genuine about seeking a permanent relationship with Him. So may we seek Him with all our hearts and we will certainly find Him. We will know when we find Him because our entire lives will change.

Have a Blessed Day! Follow Him! One Less Day to Go!

God blessed me today, when He:

_____

_____

_____

God used me today when I:

_____

_____

_____

I need to ask God to forgive me today for:

_____

_____

_____

_____

JULY 15

May the peace of our Lord Jesus Christ be with you!

> *"But go, tell His disciples and Peter, He is going ahead of you into Galilee. There you will see Him, just as He told you."*
> Mark 16: 7 NIV

This verse contains so many messages for all of us. First we must 'go and tell' that He is risen. Note how the angel separates Peter from the disciples. Peter is now the rock as said by Jesus before His death on the cross. 'There they will see Him, just as He told you.' Everything that Jesus said is coming to pass and will come to pass - just as He told us. The day of judgement is coming and we must be ready because He said so. Is that not a good reason to study the Gospels?

Have a Blessed Day! Follow Him! One Less Day to Go!

God blessed me today, when He:

_____

_____

_____

God used me today when I:

_____

_____

_____

I need to ask God to forgive me today for:

_____

_____

_____

JULY 16

May the peace of our Lord Jesus Christ be with you!

> *"Now to you who believe, this stone is precious. But to those who do not believe, 'The stone the builders rejected has become the capstone'"*
> *1 Peter 2:7 NIV*

Peter knows from personal experience that Jesus is the Rock. He also knows the impact of denying Jesus. Jesus the Rock stands between men and Heaven. The Rock will move aside and let those who believe enter freely. But to those who do not believe The Rock will be a barrier that they cannot move. I pray that we believe.

Have a Blessed Day! Follow Him! One Less Day to Go!

God blessed me today, when He:

_____

_____

_____

God used me today when I:

_____

_____

_____

I need to ask God to forgive me today for:

_____

_____

_____

_____

JULY 17

May the peace of our Lord Jesus Christ be with you!

> *"Dear children, let us not love with words or tongue but with actions and in truth."*
> *1 John 3:18 NIV*

Jesus loves us so much that He gave His life for us! True love is giving and serving without expecting anything in return. Christianity is not a faith that believes in doing good expecting good in return. Jesus, while He knew we were sinners, still decided to die for us. Our reward for loving our brothers and sisters is obedience to God's command. Our Lord knows what's in our hearts.

Have a Blessed Day! Follow Him! One Less Day to Go!

God blessed me today, when He:

_____

_____

_____

God used me today when I:

_____

_____

_____

I need to ask God to forgive me today for:

_____

_____

_____

_____

JULY 18

May the peace of our Lord Jesus Christ be with you!

> *"Do not judge, or you too will be judged. For in the same way you judge others, you will be judged, and with the measure you use, it will be measured you."*
> *Matthew 7: 1 & 2 NIV*

We judge others every day. We compare others with ourselves every day. We think lowly of others every day. It seems so easy and quick to judge. But that's not our role. God's word tells us that we must not judge. We are not qualified to judge. He is the true judge. We need to learn to pray for others instead of judging them. That's our role. So next time you are tempted to judge someone; and you will be tempted; pray for the person instead.

Have a Blessed Day! Follow Him! One Less Day to Go!

God blessed me today, when He:

_____

_____

_____

God used me today when I:

_____

_____

_____

I need to ask God to forgive me today for:

_____

_____

_____

_____

JULY 19

May the peace of our Lord Jesus Christ be with you!

> *"Be sure of this; The wicked will not go unpunished, but those who are righteous will go free."*
> *Proverbs 11:21 NIV*

Our Lord will certainly punish those who do not repent of their sins and accept Him as Lord and Savior. Romans 3:23 states, that we are all sinners - unrighteous - and that's the truth. So how do we become righteous and go free? The only way is through Jesus Christ. It is His righteousness that makes us righteous in the sight of the Lord. When God looks at a believer, He does not see our sins but He sees Jesus Christ. Thank You Jesus!

Have a Blessed Day! Follow Him! One Less Day to Go!

God blessed me today, when He:

_____

_____

_____

God used me today when I:

_____

_____

_____

I need to ask God to forgive me today for:

_____

_____

_____

_____

JULY 20

May the peace of our Lord Jesus Christ be with you!

> *"Lord, You have assigned me my portion and my cup; You have made my lot secure."*
> *Psalm 16: 5 NIV*

When Jesus gave His life for us on the cross, He assured us of a 'Godly' heritage - salvation from Hell; forgiveness of our sins and a way to Heaven.

May we learn to focus on our 'Godly' heritage(lot) that's available to us right now - a relationship with Jesus and what's waiting for us when we get to heaven. Do not allow the evil of this world to steal our heritage (lot). It is our heritage(lot) that will sustain us as we travel through this world.

Have a Blessed Day! Follow Him! One Less Day to Go!

God blessed me today, when He:

_____
_____
_____

God used me today when I:

_____
_____
_____

I need to ask God to forgive me today for:

_____
_____
_____

JULY 21

May the peace of our Lord Jesus Christ be with you!

> *"Therefore the Lord Almighty says this: "Because you have not listened to My words, I will summon all the peoples of the north and My servant Nebuchadnezzar king of Babylon," declares the Lord, "and I will bring them against this land and its inhabitants and against all surrounding nations. I will completely destroy them and make them an object of horror and scorn, and everlasting ruin.""*
> *Jeremiah 25: 8&9 NIV*

There is always some consequence when we do not listen to the word of the Lord. Are we listening to Him? Or are we so taken up with what's happening in our lives that we are deaf to His word? Listening is an active skill. It takes intention to listen; meaning we must desire to listen to our Lord. Effective sincere listening demands action by obeying the word. Too often we neglect to listen to the word of our Lord. May we develop a habit to tune into the word of our Lord and listen to Him every day or suffer the consequences.

Have a Blessed Day! Follow Him! One Less Day to Go!

God blessed me today, when He:

_____

_____

God used me today when I:

_____

_____

I need to ask God to forgive me today for:

_____

_____

JULY 22

May the peace of our Lord Jesus Christ be with you!

> *"'Martha, Martha,' The Lord answered, 'you are worried and up-*
> *set about many things, but only one thing is needed. Mary has*
> *chosen what is better, and it will not be taken away from her.'"*
> *Luke 10: 41 & 42 NIV*

Martha, like most of us, was concerned about the physical needs of herself and her guests. She was busy doing stuff, like most of us. We tend to get caught up in getting things done and neglect quiet time with our Lord. Mary on the other hand recognized the presence of her Lord and Savior and cherished the time she had with Him. That was the most important thing for her - time with Jesus. May we too be more like Mary and set aside time to kneel before our Lord and listen to Him.

Have a Blessed Day! Follow Him! One Less day to Go!

God blessed me today, when He:

_____

_____

_____

God used me today when I:

_____

_____

_____

I need to ask God to forgive me today for:

_____

_____

_____

_____

JULY 23

May the peace of our Lord Jesus Christ be with you!

> *"For great is Your love, higher than the Heavens, Your faithful-*
> *ness reaches to the skies."*
> Psalm 108:4 NIV

No love can compare with the love of our Heavenly Father. When we know, believe and experience His love; we can surely love Him more than any one or thing on this earth. It is amazing how, when we love Jesus how all other love falls in place.

Have a Blessed Day! Follow Him! One Less Day to Go!

God blessed me today, when He:

_____

_____

_____

God used me today when I:

_____

_____

_____

I need to ask God to forgive me today for:

_____

_____

_____

JULY 24

May the peace of our Lord Jesus Christ be with you!

"For the Son of Man came to seek and to save what was lost."
Luke 19:10 NIV

If there was one perfect person on Earth, Jesus would not have had to come. He came for you and me. We have strayed from His way and gotten lost. He alone could find us and bring us back. When we are on a journey and get lost we go to Google maps for direction. Similarly, life is a journey and we will get lost if we do not follow Jesus. When we get lost we can always call on Him to rescue us. That's His mission. Let us thank Him for coming for us.

Have a Blessed Day! Follow Him! One Less Day to Go!

God blessed me today, when He:

_____
_____
_____

God used me today when I:

_____
_____
_____

I need to ask God to forgive me today for:

_____
_____
_____

_____

JULY 25

May the peace of our Lord Jesus Christ be with you!

> *"When you pray, go into your room, close the door and pray to your Father who is unseen. Then your Father, who sees what is done in secret, will reward you."*
> Matthew 6:6 NIV

Our Lord wants a close one on one relationship with us. Jesus came to save us and to make Himself available to us. His instructions here are very specific. He likes face time with us and Him alone. Turn off all distractions and focus on Him totally. This should be a daily activity if you really want to get connected to Jesus. Note how many times He went to a quiet place to pray.

Have a Blessed Day! Follow Him! One Less Day to Go!

God blessed me today, when He:

_____
_____
_____

God used me today when I:

_____
_____
_____

I need to ask God to forgive me today for:

_____
_____
_____

JULY 26

May the peace of our Lord Jesus Christ be with you! Sin is not our master.

> *"Simon, Simon, Satan has asked to sift you as wheat. But I have prayed for you, Simon, that your faith may not fail, and when you have turned back, strengthen your brothers."*
> Luke 22:31 & 32 NIV

Jesus is speaking to Simon aka Peter. Satan has to ask permission from the Lord to tempt us. Read the story of Job. Jesus prays for us. He stands between us and the devil. Some might say why did Peter deny Jesus if He was praying for him. Well Peter was repentant - he cried like a baby. Then Jesus restored him to his true status - the rock. Read what Peter does when the Holy Spirit falls upon him in Acts 2: 14 to 41. One of the most powerful sermons ever preached. Jesus' prayers are always answered. That sermon started Christianity as we know it today. Amen! Read this verse one more time, but this time replace Simon with your name. Thank You Lord that You pray for us. Amen!

Have a Blessed Day! Follow Him! One Less Day to Go!

God blessed me today, when He:

_____

_____

God used me today when I:

_____

_____

I need to ask God to forgive me today for:

_____

_____

JULY 27

May the peace of our Lord Jesus Christ be with you!

> *"I keep asking that the God of our Lord Jesus Christ, the glorious Father, may give you the spirit of wisdom and revelation, so that you may know Him better."*
> *Ephesians 1:17 NIV*

Many believers know a lot about Jesus. They can tell His life story. But do we really know Him? Do we have a relationship with Him. Our Lord reveals Himself to us through His word. Our Lord is so majestic; it is impossible to get to know Him without His wisdom. How many times have you read a verse in the Bible and it does not mean anything? Then suddenly you read the same verse and you get it. That's Divine wisdom revealing His word to you. May we seek to know Him better with a desire that is never satisfied, because we can never totally get to know Him until we get to Heaven; where we will be one with Him.

Have a Blessed Day! Follow Him! One Less Day to Go!

God blessed me today, when He:

_____

_____

_____

God used me today when I:

_____

_____

_____

I need to ask God to forgive me today for:

_____

_____

_____

_____

JULY 28

May the peace of our Lord Jesus Christ be with you!

> *"He lifted me out of the slimy pit, out of the mud and mire;*
> *He set my feet on a rock and gave me a firm place to stand."*
> *Psalm 40:2 NIV*

Our Lord Jesus promised all those who believe in Him will have trials and tribulations in this world. We will fall into a pit where we feel like there is no way out. This pit could be sickness, depression, loss of a loved one etc. Our Lord will never leave us in the pit we are in right now. He will lift us up and restore us to our rightful place - children of God; heirs of the Kingdom. So brothers and sisters have faith in the Lord; seek His mercy and wait for the day when He will lift you up. Lift your hands up to Him.

Have a Blessed Day! Follow Him! One Less Day to Go!

God blessed me today, when He:

_____

_____

_____

God used me today when I:

_____

_____

_____

I need to ask God to forgive me today for:

_____

_____

_____

JULY 29

May the peace of our Lord Jesus Christ be with you!

> "I am the vine; you are the branches. If a man remains in Me
> and I in him, he will bear much fruit; apart from Me you can
> do nothing."
> John 15:5 NIV

We have a source of power freely available to us. This power sup-
plied by Jesus is unlimited. If we get connected to our Lord and stay
connected we will live productive lives. If we disconnect we can do
nothing. Those who believe know that Jesus is their sole source of
power. May we get fully connected to Jesus and produce much fruit
for Him.

Have a Blessed Day! Follow Him! One Less Day to Go!

God blessed me today, when He:

_____

_____

_____

God used me today when I:

_____

_____

_____

I need to ask God to forgive me today for:

_____

_____

_____

JULY 30

May the peace of our Lord Jesus Christ be with you!

> *"Then the eyes of those who see will no longer be closed, and*
> *the ears of those who hear will listen."*
> Isaiah 32:3 NIV

The prophet Isaiah is referring to what will happen in Heaven.
Everything will be clear for our eyes. We will be able to understand
what we see. We will not just hear but listen and understand. Our human eyes and ears will be closed but our spiritual eyes and ears will
be opened. So keep the faith my brothers and sisters and trust God
that all the unanswered questions will be answered. Let us continue
to walk by faith and not by sight.

Have a Blessed Day! Follow Him! One Less Day to Go!

God blessed me today, when He:

_____

_____

_____

God used me today when I:

_____

_____

_____

I need to ask God to forgive me today for:

_____

_____

_____

_____

JULY 31

May the peace of our Lord Jesus Christ be with you!

> *"Though the Lord is on high, He looks upon the lowly, but the proud He knows from afar."*
> *Psalm 138:6 NIV*

Pride separates us from God. No man or woman is good enough to be called the friend of God. We are His friend and children because He chooses to call us friend and sons and daughters. So let us humble ourselves in His presence and give Him thanks that He; the almighty God; will look upon us.

Have a Blessed Day! Follow Him! One Less Day to Go!

God blessed me today, when He:

_____

_____

_____

God used me today when I:

_____

_____

_____

I need to ask God to forgive me today for:

_____

_____

_____

AUGUST 1

May the peace of our Lord Jesus Christ be with you!

> *"He who has the Son, has life, he who does not have the Son of God does not have life."*
> *1 John 5:12 NIV*

To get the Son of God one has to accept Him and open your heart to receive Him. The Son of God is a free gift given to anyone who will accept Him. The evidence of having the Son is demonstrated by how we live. If we live according to His will and mirror His way then we have the Son in us. Any diversion from His commandments will indicate that we have strayed and no longer have the Son in us. May we be faithful to behave according to His will and enjoy eternal life with Him.

Have a Blessed Day! Follow Him! One Less Day to Go!

God blessed me today, when He:

_____

_____

_____

God used me today when I:

_____

_____

_____

I need to ask God to forgive me today for:

_____

_____

_____

AUGUST 2

May the peace of our Lord Jesus Christ be with you!

> *"Better the little that the righteous have, than the wealth of many wicked; for the power of the wicked will be broken, but the Lord upholds the righteous."*
> *Psalm 37:16 & 17 NIV*

May we learn to be content in the 'little' that we earn righteously and not envy the wealth of others who are disobedient to the will of God. What's important? - How much money we have in the bank; how many cars we own; how big a house we live in etc. or knowing that God holds us up and loves us. A Christian's wealth is in Heaven.

Have a Blessed Day! Follow Him! One Less Day to Go!

God blessed me today, when He:

_____

_____

_____

God used me today when I:

_____

_____

_____

I need to ask God to forgive me today for:

_____

_____

_____

AUGUST 3

May the peace of our Lord Jesus Christ be with you!

> *"So I say, live by the Spirit, and you will not gratify the desires of the sinful nature."*
> *Galatians 5:16 NIV*

The Holy Spirit guides us and protects us from our own sinful nature. How many times have you refused to do something simply because you knew it will not please the Holy Spirit? How many times have the Holy Spirit protected you from succumbing to the temptations of the evil spirit? - Countless times; for there are so many times that we are not even aware of. Read verses 17 to 21 for more insight and guidance.

Have a Blessed Day! Follow Him! One Less Day to Go!

God blessed me today, when He:

_____
_____
_____

God used me today when I:

_____
_____
_____

I need to ask God to forgive me today for:

_____
_____
_____

AUGUST 4

May the peace of our Lord Jesus Christ be with you!

> 'The Lord blessed the latter part of Job's life more than the
> first........"
> Job 42:12 NIV

The biography of Job is well known. He lost everything except his faith and trust in the Lord and 'the Lord blessed the latter part of his life more than the first.' Job is a great example of what is waiting for us in the latter part of our lives. Whatever blessings we may be receiving now; whatever trials and tribulations we may be going through right now; God, our Father who is able, will take away and replace with greater blessings in the latter part of our lives. We just need to be like Job, faithful and trusting.

Have a Blessed Day! Follow Him! One Less Day to Go!

God blessed me today, when He:

_____
_____
_____

God used me today when I:

_____
_____
_____

I need to ask God to forgive me today for:

_____
_____
_____

AUGUST 5

May the peace of our Lord Jesus Christ be with you!

> *"So then, dear friends, since you are looking forward to this, make every effort to be found spotless, blameless and at peace with Him."*
> *2 Peter 3:14 NIV*

May we continue to look forward and forget the past. If we have accepted Jesus as Lord and Savior and confess our sins, the past is forgiven and forgotten. He alone can make us spotless and blameless. It is our duty to remain in Him and pray when the day comes He will find us as He made us - spotless and blameless.

Have a Blessed Day! Follow Him! One Less Day to Go!

God blessed me today, when He:

_____
_____
_____

God used me today when I:

_____
_____
_____

I need to ask God to forgive me today for:

_____
_____
_____

_____

AUGUST 6

May the peace of our Lord Jesus Christ be with you!

> *'He guided them with the cloud by day and with the light*
> *from the fire all night.'*
> Psalm 78:14 NIV

The Israelites had the cloud by day and the fire by night to guide them and they still walked around in circles. They still complained. We have the Holy Spirit of Jesus to guide us. Let us learn to seek His wisdom and walk the straight and narrow path. May we live lives that look like we are following His steps.

Have a Blessed Day! Follow Him! One Less Day to Go!

God blessed me today, when He:

_____

_____

_____

God used me today when I:

_____

_____

_____

I need to ask God to forgive me today for:

_____

_____

_____

AUGUST 7

May the peace of our Lord Jesus Christ be with you!

> *'That if you confess with your mouth. "Jesus is Lord," and believe in your heart that God raised Him from the dead, you will be saved.'*
> *Romans 10:9 NIV*

It is not enough to say that Jesus is Lord, we must believe in our hearts without any doubt. Be careful about questioning - 'saved from what?' as some non-believers are tempted to say. Jesus Christ has paid the price for all our sins and saved us (true believers) from hell. May we confess "Jesus is Lord' every day of our lives here on Earth.

Have a Blessed Day! Follow Him! One Less Day to Go!

God blessed me today, when He:

_____
_____
_____

God used me today when I:

_____
_____
_____

I need to ask God to forgive me today for:

_____
_____
_____

_____

AUGUST 8

May the peace of our Lord Jesus Christ be with you!

> *"And having been warned in a dream not to go back to Herod,*
> *they returned to their country by another route."*
> *Matthew 2:12 NIV*

God still speaks to us today. He uses many different ways to warn us,
guide us and encourage us. Two questions we need to ask ourselves -
1. Do we listen for His voice? and 2. Do we believe that He speaks to
us? If we believe then we will seek His direction and wait to hear His
voice. How many times have you done or said something that you
never planned or felt capable. But you knew that it was the Divine
Holy Spirit of our Father leading and equipping you. May we learn to
be still and listen for His warnings and guidance.

Have a Blessed Day! Follow Him! One Less Day to Go!

God blessed me today, when He:

_____
_____
_____

God used me today when I:

_____
_____
_____

I need to ask God to forgive me today for:

_____
_____
_____
_____

AUGUST 9

May the peace of our Lord Jesus Christ be with you!

> *"For in the day of trouble He will keep me safe in His dwelling; He will hide me in the shelter of His tabernacle and set me high upon a rock."*
> Psalm 27:5 NIV

Our Lord does not promise that we will not face trials and tribulations in this world. What He does promise is that He will keep us safe; He will shelter us; He will place us where no harm can come to us. I was once on a 3 day trip where there was so much flash flooding and destruction; it made the national news. Our Father protected me and made it possible for me to complete what I went there to do and brought me home safe. This is just one example of His divine protection. He is alive and real.

Have a Blessed Day! Follow Him! One Less Day to Go!

God blessed me today, when He:

_____
_____
_____

God used me today when I:

_____
_____
_____

I need to ask God to forgive me today for:

_____
_____
_____

AUGUST 10

May the peace of our Lord Jesus Christ be with you!

> *"They will not hand you over," Jeremiah replied, "Obey the Lord by doing what I tell you. Then it will go well with you, and your life will be spared."'*
> *Jeremiah 38:26 NIV*

The Lord speaks to us through His prophets and apostles. If we obey what they tell us and what is written in the Bible, our lives will be spared. Read verses 27 and 28 to see the consequences of disobedience. May we be obedient to God's word, and His messengers.

Have a Blessed Day! Follow Him! One Less Day to Go!

God blessed me today, when He:

_____
_____
_____

God used me today when I:

_____
_____
_____

I need to ask God to forgive me today for:

_____
_____
_____

AUGUST 11

May the peace of our Lord Jesus Christ be with you!

> *"Do you see a man wise in his own eyes? There is more hope for a fool than for him."*
> *Proverbs 26:12 NIV*

Self-praise is of the devil. We who believe in Jesus know that, all of who we are, is because of Him. When we are wise it's because He makes us wise. If we seek His guidance in all things we will be wise in His eyes and according to His standards. So my brothers and sisters let us praise and give thanks to the Lord when He blesses us with wisdom.

Have a Blessed Day! Follow Him! One Less Day to Go!

God blessed me today, when He:

_____
_____
_____

God used me today when I:

_____
_____
_____

I need to ask God to forgive me today for:

_____
_____
_____

AUGUST 12

May the peace of our Lord Jesus Christ be with you!

> *"But concerning Israel He says, "All day long I have held out My hands to a disobedient and obstinate people."'*
> *Romans 10:21 NIV*

The hands of the Lord are always open for us. May we not be disobedient and obstinate. May we hold on to the hands of our Lord and receive His love, provision and protection. It's the best and safest place to be - in the hands of our Lord.

Have a Blessed Day! Follow Him! One Less Day to Go!

God blessed me today, when He:

_____
_____
_____

God used me today when I:

_____
_____
_____

I need to ask God to forgive me today for:

_____
_____
_____

AUGUST 13

May the peace of our Lord Jesus Christ be with you!

> *"I will praise You forever for what You have done; in Your name I will hope, for Your name is good. I will praise You in the presence of Your saints."*
> *Psalm 52:9 NIV*

Has God done anything for you? Is He doing anything for you right now? Are you fully aware of His presence and provision in your life? Then you have good reason to praise Him. This praise is like a song to Jesus. It should not be a secret or done only in private, but in public, especially among other believers. This is not just a 'Thank You Lord!' but a Praise God from whom all blessings flow! I pray that you will find many reasons every day, to praise the name of our Lord!

Have a blessed Day! Follow Him! One Less day to Go!

God blessed me today, when He:

_____
_____
_____

God used me today when I:

_____
_____
_____

I need to ask God to forgive me today for:

_____
_____
_____

_____

AUGUST 14

May the peace of our Lord Jesus Christ be with you!

> "Do everything without complaining or arguing, so that you may become blameless and pure, children of God without fault in a crooked and depraved generation, in which you shine like stars in the universe."
> Philippians 2:14&15 NIV

This world needs more light than ever before. We who are sons and daughters of God must make sure that our 'light' shines bright. When non-believers see us; when they talk to us; when they do business with us, may they see the light of Jesus Christ and desire to have that light. May how we carry ourselves in this world be an attraction to Jesus not a repellant. Stay connected to the power of the Holy Spirit and your light will shine bright.

Have a Blessed Day! Follow Him! One Less Day to Go!

God blessed me today, when He:

_____

_____

_____

God used me today when I:

_____

_____

_____

I need to ask God to forgive me today for:

_____

_____

_____

AUGUST 15

May the peace of our Lord Jesus Christ be with you!

> *"Whoever has My commands and obeys them, he is the one who loves Me. He who loves Me will be loved by My Father, and I too will love him and show Myself to him."*
> *John 14:21 NIV*

Knowledge of the Ten Commandments is useless without obedience. We all know what to do; the challenge is doing what we know to do every time. Jesus is telling us that we show our love for Him when we obey His word and our reward is the love of God. He will come and live in us, so that the world will see Him in us. When we have the love of Jesus, we have all that we need. Everything else is of no value compared to the love of Jesus. He died on the cross for you and me because He loves us.

Have a Blessed Day! Follow Him! One Less day to Go!

God blessed me today, when He:

_____
_____
_____

God used me today when I:

_____
_____
_____

I need to ask God to forgive me today for:

_____
_____
_____
_____

AUGUST 16

May the peace of our Lord Jesus Christ be with you!

> "For, "Whoever would love life and see good days must keep
> his tongue from evil and his lips from deceitful speech.""
> 1 Peter 3:10 NIV

Peter is one of the most qualified disciples to give us advice on our speech. Prior to his redemption, he was known for speaking out of turn and impulsive. The spoken word could do more harm than a physical blow. Once the word is spoken it is impossible to take it back. As Christians we must learn to think before we speak and make sure that our words are pleasing to God and man. This is a learned skill. May we seek the advice of Jesus before speaking.

Have a Blessed Day! Follow Him! One Less Day to Go!

God blessed me today, when He:

_____
_____
_____

God used me today when I:

_____
_____
_____

I need to ask God to forgive me today for:

_____
_____
_____

AUGUST 17

May the peace of our Lord Jesus Christ be with you!

> *"In addition to all this, take up the shield of faith, with which you can extinguish all the flaming arrows of the evil one."*
> *Ephesians 6:16 NIV*

We need stronger faith today than we had yesterday to overcome the evil that faces us every day. The closer we get to Jesus the more the devil will attack us. So my brothers and sisters may we arm ourselves with the shield of faith to protect us from the temptations of this world. I encourage you to read verses 10 to 20 of Ephesians 6. We are in a spiritual battle that we can only win with the whole armor of God. Be strong in your faith.

Have a Blessed Day! Follow Him! One Less Day to Go!

God blessed me today, when He:

_____
_____
_____

God used me today when I:

_____
_____
_____

I need to ask God to forgive me today for:

_____
_____
_____

AUGUST 18

May the peace of our Lord Jesus Christ be with you!

> *"I know that my redeemer lives, and that in the end He will*
> *stand upon the earth.'*
> Job 19:25 NIV

These are very trying times that we are experiencing. People are starving; dying from sickness; wars are being fought. Job said these words during the worst time of his life. May we too be like him and look to the face of our Lord Jesus to help us carry the burdens of caring and not being able to do anything except pray for the people who are suffering. Our Redeemer lives!

Have a Blessed Day! Follow Him! One Less Day to Go!

God blessed me today, when He:

_____

_____

_____

God used me today when I:

_____

_____

_____

I need to ask God to forgive me today for:

_____

_____

_____

AUGUST 19

May the peace of our Lord Jesus Christ be with you!

> "Remember therefore, what you have received and heard; obey it, and repent. But if you do not wake up, I will come like a thief, and you will not know at what time, I will come to you."
> Revelation 3:3 NIV

This verse is full of instruction and the consequences of disobedience. How do we remember? We select what we want to remember and repeat it until it becomes a part of us. We focus on what we want to remember. Have we heard about the Ten Commandments? Have we heard about sin and salvation? Or are we asleep to these messages. May we be awake to God's word; obey and be ready for His coming.

Have a Blessed Day! Follow Him! One Less Day to Go!

God blessed me today, when He:

_____

_____

_____

God used me today when I:

_____

_____

_____

I need to ask God to forgive me today for:

_____

_____

_____

_____

AUGUST 20

May the peace of our Lord Jesus Christ be with you!

> *"I am bringing My righteousness near, it is not far away; and My salvation will not be delayed. I will grant salvation to Zion, My splendor to Israel."*
> *Isaiah 46:13 NIV*

God's righteousness is here - Jesus Christ. His salvation is available through Jesus Christ. It's a grant, we cannot do anything to earn it - just open our hearts and receive the gift of forgiveness and salvation. Our Lord finds joy in saving His children. May we too receive His salvation with joy.

Have a Blessed Day! Follow Him! One Less Day to Go!

God blessed me today, when He:

_____

_____

_____

God used me today when I:

_____

_____

_____

I need to ask God to forgive me today for:

_____

_____

_____

AUGUST 21

May the peace of our Lord Jesus Christ be with you!

> *"Masters, provide your slaves with what is right and fair, because you know that you also have a Master in Heaven."*
> *Colossians 4:1 NIV*

I am almost certain that none of us is a master of slaves. However we may be a leader, parent, a guest at a restaurant etc. We may be in the presence of someone who is in need. Our Lord wants us to give what is fair just as He gives us way beyond our expectations.

Have a Blessed Day! Follow Him! One Less Day to Go!

God blessed me today, when He:

_____

_____

_____

God used me today when I:

_____

_____

_____

I need to ask God to forgive me today for:

_____

_____

_____

AUGUST 22

May the peace of our Lord Jesus Christ be with you!

> *"It is for freedom that Christ has set us free. Stand firm, then, and do not let yourselves be burdened again by a yoke of slavery."*
> *Galatians 5:1 NIV*

A person who was a slave will appreciate freedom more than one who was never in slavery of any sort.. Those who accept Jesus as Lord and Savior are free from the judgment; because of what Jesus did on the cross. We will only appreciate this freedom if we acknowledge our sins and confess them to Him. Now we are free, and because of His Spirit living in us, we can resist the temptations of this world. Thank You Lord for freeing us.

Have a Blessed Day! Follow Him! One Less Day to Go!

God blessed me today, when He:

_____

_____

_____

God used me today when I:

_____

_____

_____

I need to ask God to forgive me today for:

_____

_____

_____

AUGUST 23

May the peace of our Lord Jesus Christ be with you!

> *"He is not the God of the dead, but of the living, for in Him all are alive."*
> *Luke 20:38 NIV*

True believers never die. We depart from this body and this place. We get a new body and a better place in Heaven with our Father. Those who believe in Him and accept Him as Lord and Savior are alive. We are alive to Him. We are aware of His presence in our lives every day. We recognize His guidance, provision, protection and love every day. Thank God that He is our God and we are His living children.

Have a Blessed Day! Follow Him! One Less Day to Go!

God blessed me today, when He:

_____

_____

_____

God used me today when I:

_____

_____

_____

I need to ask God to forgive me today for:

_____

_____

_____

AUGUST 24

May the peace of our Lord Jesus Christ be with you!

> *"Instruct a wise man and he will be wiser still; teach a righteous man and he will add to his learning."*
> Proverbs 9:9 NIV

Learning is a continuous process. We never stop learning. Every time we read and study the Bible we learn more from it. So my brothers and sisters, seek out opportunities to learn about Jesus. Seek spiritual instruction from a Bible believing person. Find a Bible teaching church if you have not found one yet. Do not stop searching. The devil does not want us to learn more about Jesus. The day we stop growing in faith; we begin to die.

Have a Blessed Day! Follow Him! One Less Day to Go!

God blessed me today, when He:

_____

_____

_____

God used me today when I:

_____

_____

_____

I need to ask God to forgive me today for:

_____

_____

_____

_____

AUGUST 25

May the peace of our Lord Jesus Christ be with you!

> *"And again, "Praise the Lord, all you Gentiles, and sing praises to Him, all you peoples.""*
> Romans 15:11 NIV

Our Father loves to hear our voices singing His praises. Please do not make the excuse -'I cannot sing.' Jesus does not care about how we sound or if we can hold a note. All He cares about is that we sing praises to Him. So let us sing in our cars, in our bathrooms and in churches. Our singing pleases the Lord and brings joy to our own selves.

Have a Blessed Day! Follow Him! One Less Day to Go!

God blessed me today, when He:

_____
_____
_____

God used me today when I:

_____
_____
_____

I need to ask God to forgive me today for:

_____
_____
_____

AUGUST 26

May the peace of our Lord Jesus Christ be with you!

> "If I must boast, I will boast of the things that show my
> weakness."
> 2 Corinthians 11:30 NIV

Paul had so much to boast about - see verses 22 to 29, which lists
the trials and tribulations he faced and survived. Yet he only wants
to boast of his weakness because he knows that God uses the weak.
He knows that it's when we are weak we need God and seek His
face. People who boast of their strengths tend to turn off others and
set standards that seem to be impossible to achieve. Many Christians
make this mistake and non-believers turn away because they think - 'I
can never be as good as he or she.' So my brothers and sisters when
we witness let us share our weaknesses and the power of The Holy
Spirit who strengthens us. Now the non-believer can say - 'I need that
power, how can I get it?'

Have a Blessed Day! Follow Him! One Less Day to Go!

God blessed me today, when He:

_____

_____

God used me today when I:

_____

_____

I need to ask God to forgive me today for:

_____

_____

_____

AUGUST 27

May the peace of our Lord Jesus Christ be with you!

> *"For where your treasure is, there your heart will be also."*
> *Matthew 6:21 NIV*

Do not be misled into thinking treasure has to do with material things only. Treasure is anything or person you cherish or hold dearly; more than your love and devotion to Jesus Christ. We make choices in life based on what we like. If we love Jesus we will demonstrate that love by doing what He commands and not allow anything or person to get between Him and us. Watch what you favor. May we all learn to love Jesus first.

Have a Blessed Day! Follow Him! One Less Day to Go!

God blessed me today, when He:

_____
_____
_____

God used me today when I:

_____
_____
_____

I need to ask God to forgive me today for:

_____
_____
_____

_____

AUGUST 28

May the peace of our Lord Jesus Christ be with you!

> *"With the tongue we praise our Lord and Father, and with it we curse men who have been made in God's likeness."*
> James 3:9 NIV

James is one of the most direct writers of the Bible. Read verses 1 to 12. We must be very careful of the words we say when speaking to or about a fellow man or woman. My mother told me a long time ago - 'If you cannot say something good about another person, keep your mouth shut.' May we learn to be more aware of our words, that they may glorify our Father in Heaven. Someone once said - two times you should keep your mouth shut – 1, when you are under water and 2, when you are angry. Our Lord hears every word we say.

Have a Blessed Day! Follow Him! One Less Day to Go!

God blessed me today, when He:

_____
_____
_____

God used me today when I:

_____
_____
_____

I need to ask God to forgive me today for:

_____
_____
_____

_____

AUGUST 29

May the peace of our Lord Jesus Christ be with you!

> *"Then Peter, filled with the Holy Spirit, said to them, "Rulers and elders of the people! If we are being called to account today for an act of kindness shown to a cripple and are asked how he was healed, then know this, you and everyone else in Israel; It is by the name of Jesus Christ of Nazareth whom you crucified but whom God raised from the dead, that this man stands before you completely healed."'*
> *Acts 4:8-10 NIV*

This is the same Peter who a short time before denied Jesus 3 times. Big difference when he is 'filled with the Holy Spirit'. He can speak boldly and proclaim the name of Jesus Christ. He can now witness for Jesus and His healing power. I doubt he was still carrying a sword at this time. The Holy Spirit is now His strength and protection. May we too be 'filled with the Holy Spirit' and be bolder witnesses.

Have a Blessed Day! Follow Him! One Less Day to Go!

God blessed me today, when He:

_____

_____

_____

God used me today when I:

_____

_____

_____

I need to ask God to forgive me today for:

_____

_____

_____

_____

AUGUST 30

May the peace of our Lord Jesus Christ be with you!

> *"It was good for me to be afflicted so that I might learn your decrees."*
> Psalm 119:71 NIV

We will be afflicted at some time in our lives or the other. We can focus on the pain of the affliction and learn nothing or we can focus on the lessons that our Lord is teaching us and grow closer to Him. So the next time you are faced with a form of trial, look for the lessons to be learned and the pain will be easier to bare. May we too be able to say: 'It was good....'

Have a Blessed Day! Follow Him! One Less Day to Go!

God blessed me today, when He:

_____

_____

_____

God used me today when I:

_____

_____

_____

I need to ask God to forgive me today for:

_____

_____

_____

AUGUST 31

May the peace of our Lord Jesus Christ be with you!

> *"Therefore my dear friends, flee from idolatry."*
> *1 Corinthians 10:14 NIV*

May we not limit our perception of idolatry as only worshipping an image or thing. Anything; any thought, person or activity that separates us from Jesus could be an idol.

God commands us to flee from idolatry. Nothing; no shape or form could represent Jesus. So brothers and sisters, let us be on guard against the things that get between us and Jesus and flee from these things.

Have a Blessed Day! Follow Him! One Less Day to Go!

God blessed me today, when He:

_____
_____
_____

God used me today when I:

_____
_____
_____

I need to ask God to forgive me today for:

_____
_____
_____

_____

SEPTEMBER 1

May the peace of our Lord Jesus Christ be with you!

> *"And He did not do many miracles there because of their lack
> of faith."*
> Matthew 13:58 NIV

Jesus is the one who makes miracles happen. He chooses when, what
and who to do miracles for. God's word does not say that He did not
do any miracle, but that He did not do 'many', so He still did miracles
although the people did not have any faith. How strong is your faith?
Faith seems to be an ingredient for miracles. May our faith be strong
and patient. Our Lord is at work. All we need to do is believe and be
faithful.

Have a Blessed Day! Follow Him! One Less Day to Go!

God blessed me today, when He:

_____

_____

_____

God used me today when I:

_____

_____

_____

I need to ask God to forgive me today for:

_____

_____

_____

_____

SEPTEMBER 2

May the peace of our Lord Jesus Christ be with you!

> *"You need to persevere so that when you have done the will of God, you will receive what He has promised."*
> *Hebrews 10:36 NIV*

It takes a lot of faith, courage and discipline to persevere; especially when things are not going as we would like them. We are blessed with a Heavenly Father who will help us to persevere. May we seek His will in all that we do and we will receive what He has promised - eternity with Him in Heaven. Jesus has kept every promise He has made. When the devil tries to tempt us to give up on Jesus, may we turn away from the tempter and focus on our Lord. Every trial that we may face on this earth is for a short time. Persevere my brothers and sisters.

God blessed me today, when He:

_____
_____
_____

God used me today when I:

_____
_____
_____

I need to ask God to forgive me today for:

_____
_____
_____

_____

SEPTEMBER 3

May the peace of our Lord Jesus Christ be with you!

> *"In the same way, let your light shine before men, that they may see your good deeds and praise your Father in Heaven."*
> Matthew 5:16 NIV

Every one of us has a light. Some have the light shine on themselves; as if to say - 'Look at me. I am great, etc.'; others have the light shine on their fellow men and women pointing out the mistakes and sin in their lives; but a Christian's light shines to show the way to Jesus. The good deeds we do comes from the Holy Spirit; that's why he deserves all the praise and glory. Let your light shine bright my dear brothers and sisters so those who see you will get a glimpse of Jesus. Your face might be the only reflection of Jesus a person will see.

Have a Blessed Day! Follow Him! One Less Day to Go!

God blessed me today, when He:

_____
_____
_____

God used me today when I:

_____
_____
_____

I need to ask God to forgive me today for:

_____
_____
_____

_____

SEPTEMBER 4

May the peace of our Lord Jesus Christ be with you!

> *"He urged them to plead for mercy from the God of Heaven concerning this mystery, so that he and his friends might not be executed with the rest of the wise men of Babylon."*
> *Daniel 2:18 NIV*

Daniel, his friends and all the wise men of Babylon were to be executed because they could not interpret the king's dream. Daniel 'urged' his friends to not just pray for mercy but 'to plead' for mercy. We have a savior who is always available to us whenever we are threatened by evil. May we remember to go to Him and 'plead for mercy.' Our Father always answers, just as he revealed the king's dream to Daniel.

Have a Blessed Day! Follow Him! One Less Day to Go!

God blessed me today, when He:

_____
_____
_____

God used me today when I:

_____
_____
_____

I need to ask God to forgive me today for:

_____
_____
_____

_____

SEPTEMBER 5

May the peace of our Lord Jesus Christ be with you!

> *"The ax is already at the root of the trees, and every tree that does not produce good fruit will be cut down and thrown into the fire."*
> *Matthew 3:10 NIV*

John the Baptist was very direct in his preaching. Notice he does not say - anyone who does not produce plenty fruit; but 'good' fruit. Our Lord is not a numbers God. He is a quality God. He wants us to produce good fruit. We can only produce good fruit when we allow Jesus to come and dwell inside of us. Now it is by His power we are able to produce good fruit. That's our purpose to produce fruit that will please and glorify our Heavenly Father. Seek opportunity to produce good fruit every day. May we never settle for okay.

Have a Blessed Day! Follow Him! One Less Day to Go!

God blessed me today, when He:

_____

_____

_____

God used me today when I:

_____

_____

_____

I need to ask God to forgive me today for:

_____

_____

_____

_____

SEPTEMBER 6

May the peace of our Lord Jesus Christ be with you!

> *"Ants are creatures of little strength, yet they store up their*
> *food in the summer."*
> *Proverbs 30:25 NIV*

Have you ever seen an ant standing still? They seem to be moving at all times; doing something. They are known to lift things that are many times heavier than their own weight. May we learn from one of the tiniest of God's creation and always be on the move doing God's work; glorifying Him and storing up faith for when we need it. May we all be greeted with 'Well done thou good and faithful servant' when we get to Heaven.

Have a Blessed Day! Follow Him! One Less Day to Go!

God blessed me today, when He:

_____

_____

_____

God used me today when I:

_____

_____

_____

I need to ask God to forgive me today for:

_____

_____

_____

_____

SEPTEMBER 7

May the peace of our Lord Jesus Christ be with you!

> "Jesus, who is called Justus, also sends greetings. These are the
> Jews among my fellow workers for the kingdom of God, and
> they have proved a comfort to me."
> Colossians 4:11 NIV

Paul uses most of the second half of Colossians 4 to send his own greetings and share greetings from others. This must be important. We have become so busy we neglect to greet one another. Facebook can never substitute for a phone call or a personal visit. Most churches have a greeting time and people get up and shake hands. If your church does that, find someone new and say welcome.

Have a Blessed Day! Follow Him! One Less Day to Go!

God blessed me today, when He:

_____

_____

_____

God used me today when I:

_____

_____

_____

I need to ask God to forgive me today for:

_____

_____

_____

SEPTEMBER 8

May the peace of our Lord Jesus Christ be with us!

> *"If I speak in tongues of men and angels, but have not love, I am only a resounding gong, or a clanging cymbal."*
> *1 Corinthians 13:1 NIV*

1 Corinthians 13 is titled the chapter of 'Love'. We should all read this entire chapter more often. Too many people, including Christians, can impress their fellow men with their speech; but their actions or behavior do not complement their words. May we make our words kind and loving. May our speech be uplifting to those who hear and may we model the words we say.

Have a Blessed Day! Follow Him! One Less Day to Go!

God blessed me today, when He:

_____
_____
_____

God used me today when I:

_____
_____
_____

I need to ask God to forgive me today for:

_____
_____
_____

SEPTEMBER 9

May the peace of our Lord Jesus Christ be with you!

> *"The Lord Almighty has sworn, "Surely as I have planned, so it will be, and as I have purposed, so it will stand."*
> *Isaiah 14:24 NIV*

Our Lord does not make mistakes. He does not change His plans due to unforeseen circumstances. He knows everything. Nothing can surprise Him. We need to remember this about our Lord, especially when things are taking place that just does not make sense. Remember, the Lord has a plan. He is in control and His plan is for the good of those who accept Him as Lord and Savior. May we seek to live according to His plan.

Have a Blessed Day! Follow Him! One Less Day to Go!

God blessed me today, when He:

_____
_____
_____

God used me today when I:

_____
_____
_____

I need to ask God to forgive me today for:

_____
_____
_____

_____

SEPTEMBER 10

May the peace of our Lord Jesus Christ be with you!

> *"The man who eats everything must not look down on him who does not, and the man who does not eat everything must not condemn the man who does, for God has accepted him."*
> *Romans 14:3 NIV*

We humans tend to look down at others when and if they are different. People have different taste in food, clothes, life style etc. - even in worship. Most churches have a traditional service for the older folk (like me) and a contemporary service for the younger people. The thing that all believers have in common is our Savior Jesus Christ. If God accepts a person, then we too must accept him or her as a brother or sister. May we learn to accept people as they are and not as we would like them to be.

Have a Blessed Day! Follow Him! One Less Day to Go!

God blessed me today, when He:

_____
_____
_____

God used me today when I:

_____
_____
_____

I need to ask God to forgive me today for:

_____
_____
_____

SEPTEMBER 11

May the peace of our Lord Jesus Christ be with you!

> *"Therefore each of you must put off falsehood and speak truthfully to his neighbor, for we are all members of one body."*
> *Ephesians 4:25 NIV*

Jesus died for all who will believe in Him and accept Him as Lord and Savior. The devil's plan and intent is to separate the body of believers. There are so many different Christian religions, but all pray to the same God, read the same Bible, but cannot seem to unite. We tend to find fault in 'other' churches. This even happens within the walls of the church. Engaging in gossip and negative speculation only destroys the body and excites the devil. We must reunite the body of believers and look for the truth instead of fault. Let us pray that when Jesus comes back, He will find a more united body.

Have a Blessed Day! Follow Him! One Less Day to Go!

God blessed me today, when He:

_____

_____

_____

God used me today when I:

_____

_____

_____

I need to ask God to forgive me today for:

_____

_____

_____

SEPTEMBER 12

May the peace of our Lord Jesus Christ be with you!

> *"O Lord, be gracious to us; we long for You. Be our strength every morning, our salvation in time of distress."*
> Isaiah 33:2 NIV

We will have times of distress - guaranteed. If you have not yet experienced any trial or tribulation in this world; trust in the Lord, it is coming. That's why we need to keep this verse in our minds and be ready to draw on His strength in hard times. A daily morning prayer could be: 'Lord, be my strength today.'

Have a Blessed Day! Follow Him! One Less Day to Go!

God blessed me today, when He:

_____
_____
_____

God used me today when I:

_____
_____
_____

I need to ask God to forgive me today for:

_____
_____
_____

SEPTEMBER 13

May the peace of our Lord Jesus Christ be with you!

> 'You are My friends if you do what I command.'
> John 15:14 NIV

Our Lord wants us to be His friends, but He is very clear about what our responsibilities are. If we want to be God's friend, we must obey His commands. In other words we must do what pleases Him. A true friend will not do something that will hurt or embarrass his friend. I would rather be the friend of Jesus than the devil. May we seek to obey His command every day of our lives.

Have a Blessed Day! Follow Him! One Less Day to Go!

God blessed me today, when He:

_____
_____
_____

God used me today when I:

_____
_____
_____

I need to ask God to forgive me today for:

_____
_____
_____

SEPTEMBER 14

May the peace of our Lord Jesus Christ be with you!

> *"And again, when God brings His firstborn into the world, He says, "Let all God's angels worship Him."*
> *Hebrews 1:6 NIV*

Worship is an important activity of most religions. Our Lord enjoys the sound of many voices singing praises to Him; and praying to Him. Gathering with other members of the body glorifies the Father. We are His children. He loves it when His children get together to worship Him. I pray that we will all go to church and worship in body, mind and spirit. Whatever reason or circumstance that's keeping you away from going to church and worship with other believers, could only come from the devil. His job is to separate us. Jesus wants us to be united. Let us make a joyful noise this weekend and every weekend forward. This is one thing we can do for God.

Have a Blessed Day! Follow Him! One Less Day to Go!

God blessed me today, when He:

_____
_____
_____

God used me today when I:

_____
_____
_____

I need to ask God to forgive me today for:

_____
_____
_____

SEPTEMBER 15

May the peace of our Lord Jesus Christ be with you!

> *"always giving thanks to God the Father for everything, in the name of our Lord Jesus Christ."*
> *Ephesians 5:20 NIV*

It is so easy to say 'thanks' when we get what we ask for in a timely manner. But God's word tells us that we should 'always' give thanks - when He says 'no and not right now.' He is our Father. He knows what's best for us, and He wants what's best for us. So let us always give thanks to our Lord in all situations.

Have a Blessed Day! Follow Him! One Less Day to Go!

God blessed me today, when He:

_____

_____

_____

God used me today when I:

_____

_____

_____

I need to ask God to forgive me today for:

_____

_____

_____

SEPTEMBER 16

May the peace of our Lord Jesus Christ be with you!

> *"Simply let your 'Yes' be 'Yes,' and your 'No,' 'No'; anything beyond this comes from the evil one."*
> *Matthew 5:37 NIV*

Jesus is speaking to you and me - His chosen people. We all know people who can never give us a straight answer. How many times have you asked a question, and all you need is a 'yes' or 'no'; but the other person goes into a long explanation of why he or she cannot say 'yes' or 'no.' Then there are those who say 'yes' but never deliver. Jesus is saying we should be more direct in our answers. It is better to know than to be kept guessing. May we learn to say 'yes' or 'no' and keep our word. Keep it simple.

Have a Blessed Day! Follow Him! One Less Day to Go!

God blessed me today, when He:

_____
_____
_____

God used me today when I:

_____
_____
_____

I need to ask God to forgive me today for:

_____
_____
_____

_____

SEPTEMBER 17

May the peace of our Lord Jesus Christ be with you!

> *"Now you are the body of Christ, and each one of you is a part of it."*
> *1 Corinthians 12:27 NIV*

When Paul refers to the body of Christ He is talking about the church. We are the church; the body of Christ. We are His hands, His feet and His heart. As members of the body of Christ our role is to serve Him and His people. He calls us sons and daughters. He even calls us friends. So we are all connected spiritually - one family, with one Father. Read 1 Corinthians 12:28-31 for a reminder.

Have a Blessed Day! Follow Him! One Less Day to Go!

God blessed me today, when He:

_____

_____

_____

God used me today when I:

_____

_____

_____

I need to ask God to forgive me today for:

_____

_____

_____

SEPTEMBER 18

May the peace of our Lord Jesus Christ be with you!

> *"And the peace of God, which transcends all understanding, will guard your hearts and your minds in Christ Jesus."*
> *Philippians 4:7 NIV*

People who do not know Jesus will never be able to understand and appreciate the peace that comes from Him. It cannot be explained; only experienced. A believer knows where his/her peace comes from. When others are losing it and falling apart; believers can be strong because of Jesus Christ. We focus on our Lord and Savior not on the circumstances.

Have a Blessed day! Follow Him! One Less day to Go!

God blessed me today, when He:

_____

_____

_____

God used me today when I:

_____

_____

_____

I need to ask God to forgive me today for:

_____

_____

_____

SEPTEMBER 19

May the peace of our Lord Jesus Christ be with you!

> "... "We give thanks to You, Lord God Almighty, who is and
> who was, because You have taken Your great power and have
> begun to reign."'
> Revelation 11:17 NIV

May we grasp every opportunity to give thanks to our Lord who is
the same yesterday, today and tomorrow. Give thanks when He says
'yes', 'no' or 'not now.' We are truly blessed to have a God who never
changes and who rules with great power.

I pray that those of you who have not been to church recently will listen to the voice of the Lord and find a church to worship this Sunday
and every Sunday going forward.

Have a Blessed Day! Follow Him! One Less Day to Go!

God blessed me today, when He:

_____

_____

_____

God used me today when I:

_____

_____

_____

I need to ask God to forgive me today for:

_____

_____

_____

SEPTEMBER 20

May the peace of our Lord Jesus Christ be with you!

> *"For we must all appear before the judgment seat of Christ, that each one may receive what is due him for the things done while in the body, whether good or bad."*
> *2 Corinthians 5:10 NIV*

Everyone will have to face Jesus on judgment day. We are all guilty. The difference between a person who has accepted Jesus as Lord and Savior and a non-believer is, we who believe are forgiven; and our judgment will be 'Paid in full.' Let us pray for those who have not yet accepted Jesus as Lord and Savior that they too will be saved from the judgment. How much good will you be found guilty of?

Have a Blessed Day! Follow Him! One Less Day to Go!

God blessed me today, when He:

_____
_____
_____

God used me today when I:

_____
_____
_____

I need to ask God to forgive me today for:

_____
_____
_____

_____

SEPTEMBER 21

May the peace of our Lord Jesus Christ be with you!

> *"Let us not become weary in doing good, for at the proper*
> *time we will reap a harvest if we do not give up."*
> *Galatians 6:9 NIV*

Do you ever get tired of doing good and nobody seems to appreciate
what you do? That's the devil at work tempting us, using us and discouraging us from continuing to do good. We must resist this temptation and continue to do the will of the Lord. Our motive for doing
good should not be for any reward or recognition on this earth. Our
motive should always be to please God; to glorify His name and do
His will. Our reward is in Heaven.

Have a Blessed Day! Follow Him! One Less Day to Go!

God blessed me today, when He:

_____
_____
_____

God used me today when I:

_____
_____
_____

I need to ask God to forgive me today for:

_____
_____
_____

SEPTEMBER 22

May the peace of our Lord Jesus Christ be with you!

> *"And the God of all grace, who called you to His eternal glory in Christ, after you have suffered a little while, will Himself restore you and make you strong, firm and steadfast."*
> *1 Peter 5:10 NIV*

What a promise from our God who keeps His word. Any suffering that we may be going through right now is for 'a little while'. It's not permanent. Our Father has His hands on us and He is at work making us perfect as He created us in the beginning. He will establish us in His Kingdom. Our strength comes from Him and we will stand on solid ground. All we need to do in the meantime, is believe and trust Him.

Have a Blessed Day! Follow Him! One Less day to Go!

God blessed me today, when He:

_____

_____

_____

God used me today when I:

_____

_____

_____

I need to ask God to forgive me today for:

_____

_____

_____

_____

SEPTEMBER 23

May the peace of our Lord Jesus Christ be with you!

> *"I call to the Lord, who is worthy of praise; and I am saved from my enemies."*
> *Psalm 18:3 NIV*

Who are our enemies, we may ask? This could be a tough question for many of us to answer. But any person, thing or circumstance that separates us from the presence of our Father is our enemy. Let us not forget that we have a God who is more powerful than any enemy and He is always available to us. So let us call upon Him every time, not just for major battles but every battle. He is able and He will save us.

Have a Blessed Day! Follow Him! One Less Day to Go!

God blessed me today, when He:

_____

_____

_____

God used me today when I:

_____

_____

_____

I need to ask God to forgive me today for:

_____

_____

_____

SEPTEMBER 24

May the peace of our Lord Jesus Christ be with you!

> *"And now, do not be distressed and do not be angry with*
> *yourselves for selling me here, because it was to save lives that*
> *God sent me ahead of you."*
> *Genesis 45:5 NIV*

Joseph is one of my heroes in the Bible. He suffered injustice at the hands of his own brothers and then was falsely accused and placed in prison. Joseph never succumbed to the circumstances where he was placed. He trusted God and made the best of his circumstances. He believed that God had a plan and it was God who engineered his journey to Egypt to save many lives. So let us learn from Joseph and not focus on the circumstances around us but on God. Let us trust our Father to equip us to see His hand in our lives and glorify Him at all times.

Have a Blessed Day! Follow Him! One Less Day to Go!

God blessed me today, when He:

_____

_____

_____

God used me today when I:

_____

_____

_____

I need to ask God to forgive me today for:

_____

_____

_____

SEPTEMBER 25

May the peace of our Lord Jesus Christ be with you!

> *"I tell you, no! But unless you repent, you too will perish."*
> Luke 13:5 NIV

Jesus is referring to repentance of our sins. When we think of sin we tend to focus on the wrong things we do and many of us cannot find any wrong doing. Some of us may even say - well that's just a little thing, nobody was hurt. There are no little sins in the eyes of our Lord. Anything we do or say that's against His will is a sin. Then there are the things we do not do. So let us repent for the sins we know and those we do not know or perish.

Have a Blessed Day! Follow Him! One Less Day to Go!

God blessed me today, when He:

_____

_____

_____

God used me today when I:

_____

_____

_____

I need to ask God to forgive me today for:

_____

_____

_____

SEPTEMBER 26

May the peace of our Lord Jesus Christ be with you!

> *"He redeemed us in order that the blessing given to Abraham might come to the Gentiles through Christ Jesus, so that by faith we might receive the promise of the Spirit."*
> *Galatians 3:14 NIV*

The promises of God our Father are not limited to one nation. God's promises are available to anyone who would come to Him by faith and accept Him as Lord and Savior. We receive the Holy Spirit by faith and not by nationality or religion. May there be no doubt in our minds that we are children of God and heirs to His Kingdom.

Thank you Jesus, for making your blessings available to all who will believe.

Have a Blessed Day! Follow Him! One Less Day to Go!

God blessed me today, when He:

_____

_____

_____

God used me today when I:

_____

_____

_____

I need to ask God to forgive me today for:

_____

_____

_____

_____

SEPTEMBER 27

May the peace of our Lord Jesus Christ be with you!

"My steps have held to Your paths; my feet have not slipped."
Psalm 17:5 NIV

The world we live in is filled with so many temptations and distractions. The devil's mission is to get us away from God's path. That's why we need the power of the Holy Spirit to hold us up; to guide us; to discipline us and prevent us from going astray. May we pray this prayer everyday so we can stay on track with our Father in Heaven.

Have a Blessed Day! Follow Him! One Less Day to Go!

God blessed me today, when He:

_____
_____
_____

God used me today when I:

_____
_____
_____

I need to ask God to forgive me today for:

_____
_____
_____

SEPTEMBER 28

May the peace of our Lord Jesus Christ be with us!

> *"Jesus answered him, "Away from Me Satan! For it is written;*
> *"Worship the Lord your God, and serve Him only.""*
> *Matthew 4:10 NIV*

Our Lord Jesus Christ was tempted by the devil and He overcame all that the devil threw at Him. We too can say to Satan - 'In the name of Jesus Christ, get thee behind me Satan.' The moment we sense that it is the devil who is trying to talk to us, we should shut him down by repeating these powerful words - ;'In the name of Jesus Christ, get thee behind me.'

Have a Blessed Day! Follow Him! One Less day to Go!

God blessed me today, when He:

_____

_____

_____

God used me today when I:

_____

_____

_____

I need to ask God to forgive me today for:

_____

_____

_____

SEPTEMBER 29

May the peace of our Lord Jesus Christ be with you!

> *"For it has been granted to you on behalf of Christ not only to believe in Him, but also to suffer for Him."*
> *Philippians 1:29 NIV*

If we really believe in Jesus Christ we will be ready to suffer for Him. There are many believers who are giving up their lives because they are Christians today. Suffering for Jesus Christ is a different kind of suffering. It is a victorious suffering; a joyful suffering. It is a statement that says - 'We choose Jesus no matter what.' Let us pray for those who are suffering or are in danger because of their faith in Jesus.

Have a Blessed Day! Follow Him! One Less Day to Go!

God blessed me today, when He:

_____
_____
_____

God used me today when I:

_____
_____
_____

I need to ask God to forgive me today for:

_____
_____
_____

SEPTEMBER 30

May the peace of our Lord Jesus Christ be with you!

> *"Every day they continued to meet together in the temple courts. They broke bread in their homes and ate together with glad and sincere hearts, praising God and enjoying the favor of all the people. And the Lord added to their number daily those who were being saved."*
> *Acts 2:46 & 47 NIV*

The early Christians met every day. They had meals together in their homes. They did not wait for a special occasion to invite their friends and neighbors over. There is something to be said of sharing a meal with others. May we make time to meet and share a meal with our fellow believers more often. This should not be burdensome but should be something we do 'with glad and sincere hearts.'

Have a Blessed Day! Follow Him! One Less Day to Go!

God blessed me today, when He:

_____
_____
_____

God used me today when I:

_____
_____
_____

I need to ask God to forgive me today for:

_____
_____
_____
_____

OCTOBER 1

May the peace of our Lord Jesus Christ be with us!

> "Greet one another with a holy kiss. All the churches of Christ
> send greetings."
> Romans 16:16 NIV

Paul encourages us to greet one another. He is very direct and specific
- see verses 5-15 - every verse starts with 'Greet'. Today we tend to
ignore one another. Even inside churches people ignore one another.
We pass each other in corridors without a nod, or a 'good day'. May
we be a light in this world and greet one another. Don't wait until it's
too late. There is someone waiting to hear from you. Make the call
in the name of Jesus. Listen to the Holy Spirit and obey. By the way a
'holy kiss' is a plutonic kiss – on the cheek.

Have a Blessed Day! Follow Him! One Less Day to Go!

God blessed me today, when He:

_____
_____
_____

God used me today when I:

_____
_____
_____

I need to ask God to forgive me today for:

_____
_____
_____
_____

OCTOBER 2

May the peace of our Lord Jesus Christ be with you!

> *"In bringing many sons to glory, it was fitting that God, for whom and through whom everything exists, should make the author of their salvation perfect through suffering."*
> *Hebrews 2:10 NIV*

Separation is always hard and painful. When God separates us from the sins of this world it would feel as if we are suffering. But actually, we are being made perfect. Any pain or suffering we are experiencing right now is nothing compared to what Jesus experienced for us. So when pain and suffering comes, look to the face of Jesus; feel His hand on you, molding and making you perfect.

Have a Blessed Day! Follow Him! One Less Day to Go!

God blessed me today, when He:

_____
_____
_____

God used me today when I:

_____
_____
_____

I need to ask God to forgive me today for:

_____
_____
_____

_____

OCTOBER 3

May the peace of our Lord Jesus Christ be with you!

> *"Be merciful, just as your Father is merciful."*
> *Luke 6:36 NIV*

Someone is going to upset you today. Someone is going to do something bad to you and you will be tempted to feel so righteous that you will judge and condemn that person. Our Lord is telling us that is not how He wants us to behave. He wants us to be merciful just as He is merciful. So when the temptation comes, remember how much mercy our Lord has shown us, and now we can be merciful just as He is.

Have a Blessed Day! Follow Him! One Less Day to Go!

God blessed me today, when He:

_____

_____

_____

God used me today when I:

_____

_____

_____

I need to ask God to forgive me today for:

_____

_____

_____

OCTOBER 4

May the peace of our Lord Jesus Christ be with you!

> *'Listen my brothers; Has not God chosen those who are poor in the eyes of the world to be rich in faith and to inherit the kingdom He promised those who love Him?'*
> James 2:5 NIV

Whenever you are made to feel small or insignificant in this world; remember you are an heir to the Kingdom of Heaven. Worldly estates are divided among the heirs and each one gets a piece of the estate. The heirs of the Kingdom of Heaven all share the whole kingdom. To be an heir of the kingdom is a royal honor. So my brothers and sisters, take heart, when God looks at you and I He sees His heirs; adopted sons and daughters and that's what really matters.

Have a Blessed Day! Follow Him! One Less Day to Go!

God blessed me today, when He:

_____
_____
_____

God used me today when I:

_____
_____
_____

I need to ask God to forgive me today for:

_____
_____
_____

_____

OCTOBER 5

May the peace of our Lord Jesus Christ be with you!

> *"Keep your lives free from the love of money and be content with what you have, because God has said, "Never will I leave you; never will I forsake you." So we say with confidence, "The Lord is my helper; I will not be afraid. What can man do to me?"'*
> Hebrews 13:5 & 6 NIV

Nothing is wrong with having money. God knows we need money to buy what we need and He will provide. It's the love of money that gets us in trouble. May we never put our money before our Lord. May we always place Him first in our lives and remember that no matter what; He will never leave us. So when we are afraid; when we feel threatened; may we remember that 'the Lord is our helper.' We can overcome anything this world throws at us with God's help.

Have a Blessed Day! Follow Him! One Less day to Go!

God blessed me today, when He:

_____
_____
_____

God used me today when I:

_____
_____
_____

I need to ask God to forgive me today for:

_____
_____
_____
_____

OCTOBER 6

May the peace of our Lord Jesus Christ be with you!

> "Contend, O Lord, with those who contend with me; fight against those who fight against me."
> Psalm 35: 1 NIV

Like a father protects his children; so our Heavenly Father protects us, and He will defend us against anyone who will threaten to harm us. A spiritual battle is taking place right now and you and I are in the middle of it. We can only win this battle if we stand behind Jesus and call upon Him very day.

Have a Blessed Day! Follow Him! One Less Day to Go!

God blessed me today, when He:

_____
_____
_____

God used me today when I:

_____
_____
_____

I need to ask God to forgive me today for:

_____
_____
_____

OCTOBER 7

May the peace of our Lord Jesus Christ be with you!

> "My brothers, as believers in our glorious Lord Jesus Christ,
> don't show favoritism."
> James 2:1 NIV

We are always tempted to favor one person over another. Parents have their favorite child - they may not admit it, but deep down they do. Bosses have their favorite employee. We favor the rich over the poor; etc. But God's word is very direct and clear - 'Do not show favoritism.' Love one another as God loves us. This takes a lot of faith and direct action. May God fill us with His grace to treat everyone we meet, equal.

Have a Blessed day! Follow Him! One Less Day to Go!

God blessed me today, when He:

_____

_____

_____

God used me today when I:

_____

_____

_____

I need to ask God to forgive me today for:

_____

_____

_____

OCTOBER 8

May the peace of our Lord Jesus Christ be with you!

> *"For in Christ all fullness of the Deity lives in bodily form, and you have been given fullness in Christ, who is the head over every power and authority."*
> *Colossians 2:9 & 10 NIV*

When we believe, repent of our sins and accept Jesus as Lord and Savior, we receive all of Him; not some or a sample; but all of Him - His fullness. Meditate on this a lot and receive the full power of the Holy Spirit. I pray that all of us will receive His full power and use it for His glory. Open your hearts, minds and souls and stretch out your open hands and receive the fullness of Jesus Christ right now.

Have a Blessed Day! Follow Him! One Less day to Go!

God blessed me today, when He:

_____

_____

_____

God used me today when I:

_____

_____

_____

I need to ask God to forgive me today for:

_____

_____

_____

_____

OCTOBER 9

May the peace of our Lord Jesus Christ be with you!

> *"Live such good lives among the pagans that though they accuse you of doing wrong, they may see your good deeds and glorify God on the day He visits us."*
> *1 Peter 2:12 NIV*

When an unbeliever or a seeker looks upon us, what do they see? Do they see and experience anything different? Do they see an example of Jesus Christ? May the Holy Spirit that dwells is us shine bright that many will see Him through us and come to know Him. Let us show the rest of the world the good deeds of a Christian.

Have a Blessed Day! Follow Him! One Less Day to Go!

God blessed me today, when He:

_____

_____

_____

God used me today when I:

_____

_____

_____

I need to ask God to forgive me today for:

_____

_____

_____

OCTOBER 10

May the peace of our Lord Jesus Christ be with you!

> *"As the body without the spirit is dead, so faith without deeds is dead."*
> *James 2:26 NIV*

When we are filled with the Holy Spirit we live forever. Faith that is not demonstrated by good deeds is empty and useless. True faith inspires us to serve one another and even non- believers. May we all 'walk the talk' and glorify our Lord Jesus with our actions. Read Hebrews 11 for many examples of people who lived 'By Faith.'

Have a Blessed day! Follow Him! One Less Day to Go!

God blessed me today, when He:

_____

_____

_____

God used me today when I:

_____

_____

_____

I need to ask God to forgive me today for:

_____

_____

_____

OCTOBER 11

May the peace of our Lord Jesus Christ be with you!

> *"Sing to the Lord a new song, for He has done marvelous things; His right hand and His holy arm have worked salvation for him."*
> *Psalm 98:1 NIV*

The birds sing their hearts out for the Lord. They do not care if any one is listening; they sing. When we sing to the Lord, may we take a page from the bird's book and sing with all our hearts. Do not worry if you can't hold a note; God appreciates your voice. He wants to hear your voice. May we who believe proclaim all the wonders that our Lord has done and continue to do. No more secrets.

Have a Blessed Day! Follow Him! One Less day to Go!

God blessed me today, when He:

_____

_____

_____

God used me today when I:

_____

_____

_____

I need to ask God to forgive me today for:

_____

_____

_____

_____

OCTOBER 12

May the peace of our Lord Jesus Christ be with us!

> "Examine yourselves to see whether you are in the faith; test yourselves. Do you not realize that Christ Jesus is in you -- unless, of course you fail the test?'"
> 2 Corinthians 13:5 NIV

May we pass the test. Our words and actions will be a testimony of our faith. If Christ Jesus is in us, then what we say and how we behave will certainly be of Him. So before we speak; before we act; let us test ourselves by asking - 'are these words that I am about to say; are these things I am about to do, a reflection of Jesus?'

May we always speak words of encouragement and serve one another as Jesus does.

Have a Blessed Day! Follow Him! One Less Day to Go!

God blessed me today, when He:

_____
_____
_____

God used me today when I:

_____
_____
_____

I need to ask God to forgive me today for:

_____
_____
_____
_____

OCTOBER 13

May the peace of our Lord Jesus Christ be with you!

> *"Pleasant words are a honeycomb, sweet to the soul and healing to the bones."*
> Proverbs 16:24 NIV

Someone once said, 'Make your words soft and sweet, just in case you may have to eat them.' You can recall an errant email, but once the word is spoken it has its effect. You cannot take it back. My mother told me; 'Son, if you cannot say anything good, then say nothing.' May our words be a blessing to those we speak to. Let us pray that God will fill us with His Spirit so that it is His words that come out of our mouths every time. That's what followers of Christ do.

Have a Blessed Day! Follow Him! One Less Day to Go!

God blessed me today when He:

_____

_____

_____

God used me today when I:

_____

_____

_____

I need to ask God to forgive me today for:

_____

_____

_____

OCTOBER 14

May the peace of our Lord Jesus Christ be with you!

> *"Let not my heart be drawn to what is evil, to take part in wicked deeds with men who are evildoers; let me not eat of their delicacies."*
> *Psalm 141:4 NIV*

We need the protection of our Father against evil. If we think we can overcome evil without the help of our Heavenly Father; we fool ourselves and fall into the trap of overconfidence set by the devil. We know the right thing to do in the eyes of the Lord. May we learn to do what we know is right with the help of our Lord and Savior Jesus Christ.

Have a Blessed Day! Follow Him! One Less Day to Go!

God blessed me today, when He:

_____

_____

_____

God used me today when I:

_____

_____

_____

I need to ask God to forgive me today for:

_____

_____

_____

_____

OCTOBER 15

May the peace of our Lord Jesus Christ be with you!

> *"But to each one of us grace has been given as Christ appor-*
> *tioned it. This is why it says: "When He ascended on high, He*
> *led captives in His train and gave gifts to men."'*
> *Ephesians 4:7 & 8 NIV*

Jesus has given us gifts other than forgiveness of our sins and eternity with Him. We must not allow the trials and temptations of this world to rob us of the gifts that Jesus gives. There are at least seven gifts from Jesus recorded in the gospels:

(1). Rest: Matthew 11:28; (2). Keys of the Kingdom: Matthew 16: 19 (3) Power over evil spirits: Luke 10:19 (4) Living water: John 4:14 (5) Bread of Heaven: John 6:51; (6) Eternal Life: John 10:28; (7) Legacy of Peace: John 14:22; Revelation 2:26, 28 and 21:6. These are all given to anyone who will believe and receive. They are ours to accept - freely given. Receive and enjoy.

Have a Blessed day! Follow Him! One Less Day to Go!

God blessed me today, when He:

_____

_____

God used me today when I:

_____

_____

I need to ask God to forgive me today for:

_____

_____

OCTOBER 16

May the peace of our Lord Jesus Christ be with you!

> "Therefore, since through God's mercy we have this ministry,
> we do not lose heart."
> 2 Corinthians 4:1 NIV

Every believer has a specific ministry given by Jesus. This is in addition to the command to spread the Gospel. It is a joy to minister to others. If you have not yet discovered your God given ministry, then keep praying; asking God to reveal His ministry to you. 'God, how will You have me serve You today!' Then walk by faith. He will equip you. Do not hesitate when He reveals His ministry for you.

Have a Blessed Day! Follow Him! One Less Day to Go!

God blessed me today, when He:

_____
_____
_____

God used me today when I:

_____
_____
_____

I need to ask God to forgive me today for:

_____
_____
_____

OCTOBER 17

May the peace of our Lord Jesus Christ be with you!

> *"Who is wise and understanding among you? Let him share it by his good life, by deeds done in the humility that comes from wisdom."*
> *James 3:13 NIV*

We all know the right thing to do. That's knowledge. Wisdom is doing what we know is the right thing. It takes a lot of wisdom to apply the knowledge in the right way. There are many smart (knowledgeable) people who do wrong things; including you and me. If we could only learn to be wiser in our choices and actions; we will please and glorify our Father more often. Be wise in your words and deeds my dear brothers and sisters.

Have a Blessed Day! Follow Him! One Less day to Go!

God blessed me today, when He:

_____
_____
_____

God used me today when I:

_____
_____
_____

I need to ask God to forgive me today for:

_____
_____
_____

_____

OCTOBER 18

May the peace of our Lord Jesus Christ be with you!

> *"This is what the Lord Almighty says, "Give careful thought to your ways."'*
> *Haggai 1:7 NIV*

There are many eyes that observe how we behave - family, friends, co-workers, neighbors, strangers and non-believers; do they see a Christ like behavior? Do they see something different? Are our lights shining bright wherever we go? We must be fully aware of our behavior and make sure that we model the behavior that is expected of a Christian (one who belongs to Christ). Then we will attract more people to Jesus.

Have a Blessed Day! Follow Him! One Less Day to Go!

God blessed me today, when He:

_____

_____

_____

God used me today when I:

_____

_____

_____

I need to ask God to forgive me today for:

_____

_____

_____

OCTOBER 19

May the peace of our Lord Jesus Christ be with you!

> *"Turn from evil and do good; seek peace and pursue it."*
> *Psalm 34:14 NIV*

Jesus is peace. When the angels announced His birth it was 'Peace on Earth, goodwill to men.' If we have His Holy Spirit in us we will definitely seek peace. Seeking peace is a command from God. If we believers do not seek peace, then we are no different from the non-believers. The world we live in needs more peace. May we all be peacemakers, by God's grace.

Have a Blessed Day! Follow Him! One Less Day to Go!

God blessed me today, when He:

_____

_____

_____

God used me today when I:

_____

_____

_____

I need to ask God to forgive me today for:

_____

_____

_____

OCTOBER 20

May the peace of our Lord Jesus Christ be with you!

> *"Command those who are rich in this present world not to be arrogant nor to put their hope in wealth, which is so uncertain, but to put their hope in God, who richly provides us with everything for our enjoyment."*
> *1 Timothy 6:17 NIV*

Rich in this world is such a relative term. Many of us are so rich we are not aware of it. We tend to focus on what we do not have instead of what we do have. God provides everything we 'need for our enjoyment.' So may we be wise enough to enjoy the blessings that come from the Lord and not be envious of others who may appear to have more. No matter how much we have in this world; more is waiting for us in Heaven.

Have a Blessed Day! Follow Him! One Less Day to Go!

God blessed me today, when He:

_____
_____
_____

God used me today when I:

_____
_____
_____

I need to ask God to forgive me today for:

_____
_____
_____
_____

OCTOBER 21

May the peace of our Lord Jesus Christ be with you!

"Glory to His holy name; let the hearts of those that seek the
Lord rejoice."
Psalm 105:3 NIV

We find what we look for. God gave us the free will to choose. We can choose to seek after worldly matters and neglect the Lord; or we can seek the Lord in all things and rejoice. It is a joy to find the Lord and accept Him as Lord and Savior. It is a time of rejoicing. May we choose to rejoice in the presence of the Lord.

Have a Blessed day! Follow Him! One Less Day to Go!

God blessed me today, when He:

_____

_____

_____

God used me today when I:

_____

_____

_____

I need to ask God to forgive me today for:

_____

_____

_____

OCTOBER 22

May the peace of our Lord Jesus Christ be with us!

> *"But the wisdom that is from heaven is first of all pure; then peace loving, considerate, submissive, full of mercy and good fruit, impartial and sincere."*
> *James 3:17 NIV*

This verse reminds me of the Beatitudes (Matthew 5: 3-10) and Galatians 5:22 (the fruit of the spirit). When our source of wisdom is from Jesus, these are the characteristics of our lives. Wisdom is seen by our words and actions. May our words and actions represent the wisdom that comes from Jesus.

Have a Blessed Day! Follow Him! One Less Day to Go!

God blessed me today, when He:

_____
_____
_____

God used me today when I:

_____
_____
_____

I need to ask God to forgive me today for:

_____
_____
_____

_____

OCTOBER 23

May the peace of our Lord Jesus Christ be with you!

> *"Praise the Lord, all His works everywhere in His dominion.*
> *Praise the Lord, O my soul."*
> *Psalm 103:22 NIV*

A Holy and spiritual habit is to stop each day and praise the Lord. One Sunday afternoon a bird came close to my window and I could see him and hear him whistle his heart out. He gave it his all. He did not care who was listening; who appreciated his song. He just went about doing what he was created to do. May we be like the birds that whistle in praise to our Lord - may we pause every day and sing praises to Him with all our heart and soul. Do not allow the evil of this world to steal our joy of praising our Father.

Have a Blessed Day! Follow Him! One Less Day to Go!

God blessed me today, when He:

_____
_____
_____

God used me today when I:

_____
_____
_____

I need to ask God to forgive me today for:

_____
_____
_____
_____

OCTOBER 24

May the peace of our Lord Jesus Christ be with you!

"There remains, then, a Sabbath rest for the people of God. For anyone who enters God's rest also rests from his own work, just a God did from His. Let us, therefore, make every effort to enter that rest, so that no one will fall by following their example of disobedience."
Hebrews 4: 9, 10 & 11 NIV

We worship and serve a God who thinks of everything. He even demands that we rest. If we decide not to rest then we disobey our Lord and will suffer the consequences. The human body was created strong, but to remain strong, we must rest, both physically and spiritually. If you have not tried quiet time; a time of silence; doing nothing but staying in the presence of God; try it and reap the benefits. To rest is not being lazy. It's a time to recharge the body and spirit.

Have a Blessed Day! Follow Him! One Less Day to Go!

God blessed me today, when He:

_____

_____

God used me today when I:

_____

_____

I need to ask God to forgive me today for:

_____

_____

_____

_____

OCTOBER 25

May the peace of our Lord Jesus Christ be with you!

"Blessed is the man who perseveres under trial, because when he has stood the test, he will receive the crown of life that God has promised to those who love Him."
James 1:12 NIV

Jesus did not promise us a life without any trial or trouble. In fact as our faith and trust in Jesus grows; the devil will come after us with a greater effort. It is a blessing to continue to trust in Jesus; to be faithful to His way and not give in to the evils of this world. Our reward for persevering is 'the crown of life' which is eternal life with Jesus. That's what's waiting for us. Nothing in this world comes close to what is waiting for us in Heaven. We will be stronger after every trial.

Have a Blessed Day! Follow Him! One Less Day to Go!

God blessed me today, when He:

_____
_____
_____

God used me today when I:

_____
_____
_____

I need to ask God to forgive me today for:

_____
_____
_____
_____

OCTOBER 26

May the peace of our Lord Jesus Christ be with you!

> *"A righteous man may have many troubles, but the Lord delivers him from them all."*
> *Psalm 34:19 NIV*

Jesus never promised us that we would not have any trouble in this world.(Sounds familiar?) In fact He assured us that we would be prosecuted just because we claim Him as Lord and Savior. What He did promise us is that He will be with us at all times - good and bad. He will rescue us from all troubles as long as we remember to call upon Him. That's a major difference between a righteous man and a non-righteous man - a righteous man knows that he is only righteous because of the grace of the Lord and he calls on the Lord many times every day. That's what keeps him righteous.

Have a Blessed Day! Follow Him! One Less Day to Go!

God blessed me today, when He:

_____

_____

_____

God used me today when I:

_____

_____

_____

I need to ask God to forgive me today for:

_____

_____

_____

OCTOBER 27

May the peace of our Lord Jesus Christ be with you!

> *"If anyone considers himself religious and yet does not keep a tight rein on his tongue, he deceives himself and his religion is worthless."*
> James 1:26 NIV

How many times have we said things we did not intend to say, or had to apologize because we said something that did not come out as we intended. A Christian must learn to think before speaking and make sure that his/her words are encouraging and constructive. Someone once said, 'Make your words soft and sweet, just in case you have to eat them.' May we learn to speak words that are pleasing to God. Remember He hears everything.

Have a Blessed Day! Follow Him! One Less Day to Go!

God blessed me today, when He:

_____

_____

_____

God used me today when I:

_____

_____

_____

I need to ask God to forgive me today for:

_____

_____

_____

_____

OCTOBER 28

May the peace of our Lord Jesus Christ be with you!

> *"Bear with each other and forgive whatever grievances you may have against one another. Forgive as the Lord forgave you."*
> *Colossians 3:13 NIV*

Forgiveness is one of the biggest differences of the Christian faith. Our Lord asks us to forgive as He forgave us. Do you feel forgiven? When we feel forgiven for our sins then we can forgive others. This is not easy. We need the grace of our Lord Jesus to be able to forgive those who hurt us. May our Father bless us with the power to forgive.

Have a Blessed Day! Follow Him! One Less Day to Go!

God blessed me today, when He:

_____

_____

_____

God used me today when I:

_____

_____

_____

I need to ask God to forgive me today for:

_____

_____

_____

OCTOBER 29

May the peace of our Lord Jesus Christ be with you!

> *"There will be trouble and distress for every human being who does evil; first for the Jew then for the Gentile, but glory, honor and peace for everyone who does good; first for the Jew then for the Gentile. For God does not show favoritism."*
> *Romans 2:9 - 11 NIV*

We all know what is evil and what is good in the eyes of our Lord. The consequences of doing evil are 'trouble and distress'; mildly put. The rewards of doing good are - 'glory, honor and peace.' The important thing here is not who comes first or second but who does good or evil. Our Lord does not show favoritism. I pray that we will all choose to do what's good in the eyes of the Lord and reap the rewards.

Have a Blessed Day! Follow Him! One Less Day to Go!

God blessed me today, when He:

_____

_____

_____

God used me today when I:

_____

_____

_____

I need to ask God to forgive me today for:

_____

_____

_____

OCTOBER 30

May the peace of our Lord Jesus Christ be with you!

> *"He who has an ear, let him hear what the Spirit says to the churches. He who overcomes will not be hurt at all by the second death."*
> *Revelation 2:11 NIV*

We all have ears to hear, but do we listen? When God's word says 'let him hear', it means we must be active about hearing and listen to His word. When we listen we take action and we are able to overcome the temptations of this world. The devil will try his best to deceive us. We must not listen to his voice but the voice of Jesus. Repent and obey. Now we will not die the second death. The first death is the death of the physical body. Those who repent and accept Jesus as Lord and Savior will not die the spiritual death but will spend eternity with Jesus in Heaven.

Have a Blessed Day! Follow Him! One Less Day to Go!

God blessed me today, when He:

_____
_____
_____

God used me today when I:

_____
_____
_____

I need to ask God to forgive me today for:

_____
_____
_____

OCTOBER 31

May the peace of our Lord Jesus Christ be with you!

> *"Why are you downcast, O my soul? Why so disturbed within*
> *me? Put your hope in God, for I will yet praise Him, my Savior*
> *and my God."*
> *Psalm 42:11 NIV*

When we are faced with the trials and temptations of this world, we tend to get anxious, sad, worrisome and disturbed. We may even question God. These are testing times. These are the times when we must put our hope in the Lord and praise Him in all things. I can't tell you how many times I have had to ask for forgiveness for being sad and anxious. Our Lord always comes through for us. So, no matter what you are going through right now, put your hope in God and praise Him. Then wait and see how He rescues and comforts you.

Have a Blessed Day! Follow Him! One Less Day to Go!

God blessed me today, when He:

_____

_____

_____

God used me today when I:

_____

_____

_____

I need to ask God to forgive me today for:

_____

_____

_____

NOVEMBER 1

May the peace of our Lord Jesus Christ be with you!

> *"Live as free men, but do not use your freedom as a cover-up for evil; live as servants of God."*
> *1 Peter 2:16 NIV*

Forgiveness does not give us license to sin. We who believe are free of the condemnation of our sins because Jesus died in our place. Our response is to live as servants of God. A good servant knows the will of the Master and obeys. A good servant glorifies the Master at all times. We must choose - servants of God or the devil. Choose wisely my dear brothers and sisters.

Have a Blessed Day! Follow Him! One Less Day to Go!

God blessed me today, when He:

_____

_____

_____

God used me today when I:

_____

_____

_____

I need to ask God to forgive me today for:

_____

_____

_____

NOVEMBER 2

May the peace of our Lord Jesus Christ be with you!

> *"Your sun will never set again, and your moon will wane no more; the Lord will be your everlasting light, and your days of sorrow will end."*
> *Isaiah 60:20 NIV*

This is the promise of our Lord and His blessing to His people. So when things are not going, as you would like; when you are sad; hold on to His promise. A person who has experienced darkness will have a greater appreciation of light. He will be our everlasting light. Our hope is that we will spend eternity with our Father. Thank you Lord for Your assurance. Forgive us when we doubt.

Have a Blessed Day! Follow Him! One Less Day to Go!

God blessed me today, when He:

_____
_____
_____

God used me today when I:

_____
_____
_____

I need to ask God to forgive me today for:

_____
_____
_____

_____

NOVEMBER 3

May the peace of pour Lord Jesus Christ be with you!

> *"May Your unfailing love rest upon us, O Lord, even as we put our hope in You."*
> *Psalm 33:22 NIV*

Just think for a moment - what will it be like without the unfailing love of our Lord? What will it be like if we have no hope? There are many who still do not believe in God and place their hope in themselves and their possessions. We need to continue sharing the Gospel and invite more non-believers to experience God's love and forgiveness. This verse could be a good verse to include in our daily prayers.

Have a Blessed Day! Follow Him! One Less Day to Go!

God blessed me today, when He:

_____
_____
_____

God used me today when I:

_____
_____
_____

I need to ask God to forgive me today for:

_____
_____
_____

NOVEMBER 4

May the peace of our Lord Jesus Christ be with you!

> *"Whoever believes in Him is not condemned, but whoever does not believe stands condemned already because he has not believed in the name of God's one and only Son."*
> *John 3:18 NIV*

Many Christians still struggle with the assurance of freedom from condemnation. The Gospel of John tells us in the present tense that we who believe 'is not condemned' If there is condemnation then Jesus died for nothing. The day of judgment is coming and non-believers will suffer the consequences of their choice. Our belief will influence our actions, which will in turn impact the results we gain. May we who believe act as if we are not condemned and reap the rewards of eternity with Jesus Christ.

Have a Blessed Day! Follow Him! One Less Day to Go!

God blessed me today, when He:

_____
_____
_____

God used me today when I:

_____
_____
_____

I need to ask God to forgive me today for:

_____
_____
_____
_____

NOVEMBER 5

May the peace of our Lord Jesus Christ be with you!

> *"One of those days Jesus went out into the hills to pray, and spent the night praying to God."*
> *Luke 6:12 NIV*

The prayer life of Jesus is an example for us to follow. He always prayed to His Father before doing anything. He chose the 12 disciples after this night of prayer. He gave thanks to God before feeding the 5,000. He prayed in the garden of Gethsemane on the night He was betrayed. These are just a few examples. If we too could learn to pray before we do anything, our lives will be much more stress free. We would make better decisions. Our lives will be more glorifying to the Lord. Let us pray without ceasing.

Have a Blessed Day! Follow Him! One Less day to Go!

God blessed me today, when He:

_____
_____
_____

God used me today when I:

_____
_____
_____

I need to ask God to forgive me today for:

_____
_____
_____

_____

NOVEMBER 6

May the peace of our Lord Jesus Christ be with you!

> *"May my cry come before You, O Lord, give me understanding according to Your word."*
> *Psalm 119:169 NIV*

There is so much stuff taking place that I have a hard time understanding. How about you? Thank God He knows everything and can explain everything to us if we seek His wisdom. He will explain everything to us but in His time. So if you are experiencing something right now that just does not make sense; cry out to the Lord for understanding, then wait on Him. This is what faith and trust in God is all about.

Have a Blessed Day! Follow Him! One Less Day to Go!

God blessed me today, when He:

_____

_____

_____

God used me today when I:

_____

_____

_____

I need to ask God to forgive me today for:

_____

_____

_____

NOVEMBER 7

May the peace of our Lord Jesus Christ be with you!

> "So Paul and Barnabas spent considerable time there. speaking boldly for the Lord, who confirmed the message of His grace by enabling them to do miraculous signs and wonders."
> Acts 14:3 NIV

When we speak 'for' the Lord; when we act 'for' the Lord, he will bless our words and our actions. When we speak or act on our own accord, we cannot expect His blessings. He knows who speaks for Him and who does not. He will validate those who speak and do 'for' Him with amazing results. So if you are speaking and acting for Him and have not yet seen the amazing results, do not give up. Keep sowing the seeds.

Have a Blessed Day! Follow Him! One Less Day to Go!

God blessed me today, when He:

_____

_____

_____

God used me today when I:

_____

_____

_____

I need to ask God to forgive me today for:

_____

_____

_____

_____

NOVEMBER 8

May the peace of our Lord Jesus Christ be with you!

> *"To one He gave five talents of money, to another two talents,*
> *and to another one talent, each according to his ability."*
> *Matthew 25:15 NIV*

Thanksgiving day in the USA is a few days away. It is one of the biggest holiday celebrations here. As we get ready to celebrate let us focus on what we have, and not on what others have. God knows you and me better than we know ourselves. It is He who created us. He will never give us more than we can handle. If you read the parable, the two servants who got 5 and 2 talents focused on what they got and made the best use of it, doubling their talents. The one who got 1 talent buried it. Do not bury your gifts. Let us use what God has given to us to glorify Him to the best of our abilities.

Have a Blessed Day! Follow Him! One Less Day to Go!

God blessed me today, when He:

_____
_____
_____

God used me today when I:

_____
_____
_____

I need to ask God to forgive me today for:

_____
_____
_____
_____

NOVEMBER 9

May the peace of our Lord Jesus Christ be with you!

> *"This is love for God; to obey His commands. And His commands are not burdensome."*
> *1 John 5:3 NIV*

If you are wondering whether you really love God or not; if there is any doubt in your mind, then this verse speaks to you. I love how our Lord makes this so simple for us. If we love Him we will obey His commands. His commands are not burdensome because our obedience is inspired by love for Him. Anything done with love is joyful.

Have a Blessed Day! Follow Him! One Less Day to Go!

God blessed me today, when He:

_____

_____

_____

God used me today when I:

_____

_____

_____

I need to ask God to forgive me today for:

_____

_____

_____

NOVEMBER 10

May the peace of our Lord Jesus Christ be with you!

> *"For we know in part and we prophesy in part, but when perfection comes the imperfect disappears."*
> *1 Corinthians 13:9 & 10 NIV*

We can only speak about what the Lord reveals to us. There will always be unexplainable mysteries about God. If we knew everything there is to know about God then He would not be infinite. Paul tells us that a day is coming when we will be restored to what God's original intention was when He created us in His image. Then we will know everything there is to know about God. Meanwhile we walk by faith and trust Him.

Have a Blessed Day! Follow Him! One Less Day to Go!

God blessed me today, when He:

_____

_____

_____

God used me today when I:

_____

_____

_____

I need to ask God to forgive me today for:

_____

_____

_____

NOVEMBER 11

May the peace of our Lord Jesus Christ be with you!

> *"Let us not give up meeting together, as some are in the habit of doing, but let us encourage one another -- and all the more as you see the Day approaching."*
> *Hebrews 10:25 NIV*

Paul is encouraging us to gather in numbers to worship and encourage one another. Some of us make excuses for not going to church regularly. I wonder what their answer will be on that Day, when God Himself asks - 'Why did you not go to church on a regular basis?' It seems that we are so caught up and distracted by what's going on in the world, we do not have time for communal worship. Worship pleases God. So when we do not go, who are we pleasing? Worship is one of the few things we can do for God.

Have a Blessed day! Follow Him! One Less Day to Go!

God blessed me today, when He:

_____
_____
_____

God used me today when I:

_____
_____
_____

I need to ask God to forgive me today for:

_____
_____
_____
_____

NOVEMBER 12

May the peace of our Lord Jesus Christ be with you!

> "We all fell to the ground, and I heard a voice saying to me
> in Aramaic, 'I am Jesus, whom you are persecuting,' the Lord
> replied."
> Acts 26:14 NIV

Paul liked to tell this story of how Jesus confronted him while he was
on his way to Damascus to persecute the Christians. Jesus stood up
for them at the time and He stands up for us today. When we are persecuted because of Him, He takes that personally. What a Savior who
will always put Himself in our place. In other words our Lord is saying
- if you harm My people, you harm Me and will have to deal with Me.

May we be confident of our Lord's protection from all forms of evil.
He is our shield. So if you are feeling attacked and persecuted right
now, do not be afraid. Jesus is right there beside you and He will deal
with your persecutors.

Have a Blessed Day! Follow Him! One Less Day to Go!

God blessed me today, when He:

_____

_____

God used me today when I:

_____

_____

I need to ask God to forgive me today for:

_____

_____

_____

NOVEMBER 13

May the peace of our Lord Jesus Christ be with you! I pray that we will glorify our Lord with every thought, word and action we take today and every day.

> *"Do not be afraid, for I am with you; I will bring your children from the east and gather you from the west."*
> *Isaiah 43:5 NIV*

The lesson for us here is 'Do not be afraid, for I am with you.' If we really believe that Jesus is with us at all times, we will never be afraid. Just as our Lord promised the Israelites to protect them and provide for them; He is making the same promise to you and me. So let us not be afraid; simply because we know that our Lord is with us and nothing is bigger or stronger than our God.

Have a Blessed Day! Follow Him! One Less Day to Go!

God blessed me today, when He:

_____
_____
_____

God used me today when I:

_____
_____
_____

I need to ask God to forgive me today for:

_____
_____
_____

_____

NOVEMBER 14

May the peace of our Lord Jesus Christ be with you!

> *"He who keeps the law is a discerning son, but a companion of gluttons disgraces his father."*
> *Proverbs 28:7 NIV*

Obedience to God's law pleases Him. Disobedience disgraces Him. We do have a choice. We can either obey God's laws and glorify Him or disobey and disgrace Him. We all know what is expected of us, yet we stray and do what we know we should not. Thank God we have a forgiving Father. May we learn to be obedient at all times. When we disobey we glorify the devil. Do we really want to do that?

Have a Blessed Day! Follow Him! One Less Day to Go!

God blessed me today, when He:

_____

_____

_____

God used me today when I:

_____

_____

_____

I need to ask God to forgive me today for:

_____

_____

_____

NOVEMBER 15

May the peace of our Lord Jesus Christ be with you!

> *"Never lacking in zeal, but keep your spiritual fervor, serving the Lord."*
> *Romans 12:11 NIV*

Believers give their all in everything they do because they serve the Lord, not man. Every one of us is given a responsibility by our Father. Our job is to do what He commands to the best of our ability. Do not allow, other people or circumstances to prevent you from serving the Lord to the best of your ability. He will carry you when you feel weak. He will remove barriers from your way. Our job is to be zealous and full of 'spiritual fervor.'

Have a Blessed day! Follow Him! One Less Day to Go!

God blessed me today, when He:

_____
_____
_____

God used me today when I:

_____
_____
_____

I need to ask God to forgive me today for:

_____
_____
_____

_____

NOVEMBER 16

May the peace of our Lord Jesus Christ be with all of you!

> *"Meanwhile, when a crowd of many thousands had gathered, so that they were trampling on one another, Jesus began to speak first to his disciples, saying:"Be on your guard against the yeast of the Pharisees, which is hypocrisy. There is nothing concealed that will not be disclosed, or hidden that will not be made known."'*
> *Luke 12: 1 & 2 NIV*

We must be on guard so that we too will not become hypocrites. We must not just talk the talk but walk the talk. God knows everything and sees everything. He knows our thoughts. He knows what we will say before we even say it. We serve God not man. We may be able to fool man for a short time, but we can never fool God. When we come to a place in our faith and knowledge of an all-knowing God, we have no choice but to be obedient to His way. May all our hearts be clean and clear of any hate.

Have a Blessed Day! Follow Him! One Less Day to Go!

God blessed me today, when He:

_____

_____

God used me today when I:

_____

_____

I need to ask God to forgive me today for:

_____

_____

_____

NOVEMBER 17

May the peace of our Lord Jesus Christ be with you!

> *"The fear of the Lord is pure, enduring forever. The ordinances of the Lord are sure and altogether righteous. They are more precious than gold, than much pure gold; they are sweeter than honey, than honey from the comb."*
> *Psalm 19:9 & 10 NIV*

This world is full of distractions that will tempt us to disobey God's word. But a true believer knows that obeying God's word is the most precious thing that can happen. Everything in this world is less than what God has waiting for us in Heaven. So brothers and sisters, may we be strong in our faith and obey our Father. May we always stand behind His shield against the evils of this world.

Have a Blessed Day! Follow Him! One Less Day to Go!

God blessed me today, when He:

_____
_____
_____

God used me today when I:

_____
_____
_____

I need to ask God to forgive me today for:

_____
_____
_____

_____

NOVEMBER 18

May the peace of our Lord Jesus Christ be with you!

> *"One thing I ask of the Lord, this is what I seek, that I may dwell in the house of the Lord all the days of my life, to gaze upon the beauty of the Lord and to seek Him in His temple."*
> *Psalm 27:4 NIV*

Psalm 27 is one of my favorites Psalms. Can we be like David? All he wants is to be with the Lord all the days of his life; just to gaze on the beauty of the Lord. Many may say. well that's boring. It will be boring from a worldly perspective but when we receive our new heart and mind, we will find infinite joy in simply 'gazing upon the beauty of the Lord.' So may we seek this one thing that's more precious than anything on earth - eternal life with Jesus.

Have a Blessed Day! Follow Him! One Less Day to Go!

God blessed me today, when He:

_____

_____

_____

God used me today when I:

_____

_____

_____

I need to ask God to forgive me today for:

_____

_____

_____

_____

NOVEMBER 19

May the peace of our Lord Jesus Christ be with you!'

> *"But Stephen, full of the Holy Spirit, looked up to Heaven and saw the glory of God, and Jesus standing at the right hand of God. "Look," he said, "I see Heaven open and the Son of Man standing at the right hand of God."'*
> Acts 7: 55 & 56 NIV

The Bible is full of examples of what happens when people become 'full of the Holy Spirit.' Miracles happen when we are 'full of the Holy Spirit'. History records how Christians die a peaceful death. This can only happen if we are 'full of The Holy Spirit'. We will see things that no one else can see. God's word will become clearer to us. We will gain strength to be obedient and not yield to temptations. So how do we get 'full of The Holy Spirit'. Jesus said, just open your heart and let Him in. So my beloved brothers and sisters let us open our hearts and let The Holy Spirit occupy every nook and cranny of our being; leaving no room for any other. Then watch what He does with and through us. We can now be strong even in the face of death.

Have a Blessed Day! Follow Him! One Less Day to Go!

God blessed me today, when He:

_____

_____

God used me today when I:

_____

_____

I need to ask God to forgive me today for:

_____

_____

_____

NOVEMBER 20

May the peace of our Lord Jesus Christ be with you!

> *"The Lord is my strength and my shield; my heart trusts in Him, and I am helped. My heart leaps for joy and I will give thanks to Him in song."*
> *Psalm 28: 7 NIV*

Those who stand behind the shield of the Lord will fear no evil for they know that they are well protected. We can say with our mouths that the Lord is our strength and shield, but we must also trust Him in our hearts and believe that our help comes from Him. Then our hearts will rejoice in the confidence that he is with us. Don't worry if you cannot sing. Our Lord does not listen for notes or tones; He listens to our hearts for sincerity. So let us praise Him!

Have a Blessed Day! Follow Him! One Less Day to Go!

God blessed me today, when He:

_____

_____

_____

God used me today when I:

_____

_____

_____

I need to ask God to forgive me today for:

_____

_____

_____

_____

NOVEMBER 21

May the peace of our Lord Jesus Christ be with you!

> *"Once more the humble will rejoice in the Lord; the needy will rejoice in the Holy One of Israel."*
> *Isaiah 29:19 NIV*

Isaiah is prophesying of the day when the Lord comes, the day that no one knows exactly when. If you read all of Chapters 29 and 30; it could be scary. This particular verse highlights two qualities - 'humility' and 'needy.' May we humble ourselves in the eyes of the Lord and my we be always 'needy' of His grace. When that day comes I pray that we will be the ones rejoicing.

Have a Blessed Day! Follow Him! One Less Day to Go!

God blessed me today, when He:

_____

_____

_____

God used me today when I:

_____

_____

_____

I need to ask God to forgive me today for:

_____

_____

_____

NOVEMBER 22

May the peace of our Lord Jesus Christ be with you!

> *"Then I acknowledged my sin to you and did not cover up my*
> *iniquity. I said, "I will confess my transgressions to the Lord"-*
> *-- and You forgave the guilt of my sin."*
> *Psalm 32:5 NIV*

Our Lord just does not forgive all sins. He forgives confessed sins. Too many 'Christians' try to debate their purity with God. We forget that God sees all and knows all. It is futile to hide anything from God. So brothers and sisters let us all confess our sins to the Lord and He will forgive us. Jesus made it possible for you and me to kneel in God's presence and confess our sins directly to Him.

Have a Blessed Day! Follow Him! One Less Day to Go!

God blessed me today, when He:

_____

_____

_____

God used me today when I:

_____

_____

_____

I need to ask God to forgive me today for:

_____

_____

_____

NOVEMBER 23

May the peace of our Lord Jesus Christ be with you!

> *"Then I looked and there before me was the Lamb, standing on Mount Zion, and with Him 144,000 who had His name and His Father's name written on their foreheads."*
> *Revelation 14:1 NIV*

Many interpret this verse to mean that only 144,000 will be saved and go to Heaven to be with Jesus. But if we read more of chapter 14, we will learn that this is a special 144,000. See verse 4. Revelation 7-9. John talks about a 'multitude that no one can count.' Jesus never said that He came to save 144,000. He said He came to save all who will believe, confess their sins and accept Him as Lord and Savior. Revelation 22:17 says: 'The Spirit and the bride say, "Come!" Whoever is thirsty, let him come, and whoever wishes, let him take the free gift of the water of life." So do not be fooled; know that there is a place for you and me in Heaven.

Have a Blessed Day! Follow Him! One Less Day to Go!

God blessed me today, when He:

_____
_____
_____

God used me today when I:

_____
_____
_____

I need to ask God to forgive me today for:

_____
_____
_____

NOVEMBER 24

May the peace of our Lord Jesus Christ be with you!

> "All those gathered here will know that it is not by sword or spear that the Lord saves; for the battle is the Lord's. and He will give all of you into our hands."
> 1 Samuel 17:47 NIV

Read the entire chapter 17 of 1 Samuel. Most of us are acquainted with the story of David and Goliath. We are faced with some form of a Goliath today - sometimes every day and sometimes occasionally. Let us learn from David. He went to battle against unbelievable odds with no armor, but his faith and trust was in Jesus. Our Lord is our shield and sword. If we could only learn to trust in Him and have a faith like David, we will be victorious by His Grace. So whatever is bothering you, or hurting you, or causing you anxiety right now - give it up to Jesus. He is able!

Have a Blessed Day! Follow Him! One Less Day to Go!

God blessed me today, when He:

_____

_____

_____

God used me today when I:

_____

_____

_____

I need to ask God to forgive me today for:

_____

_____

_____

NOVEMBER 25

May the peace of our Lord Jesus Christ be with you!

> *'..giving thanks to the Father, who has qualified you to share in the inheritance of the saints in the kingdom of light.'*
> *Colossians 1:12 NIV*

We have so much to be thankful for in this world. But there are so much greater blessings ahead of us because our God 'has qualified us to share in the inheritance of the saints.' Nothing on this earth can compare to what is waiting for us 'in the kingdom of light.' So while it is good to give thanks; and this should not just be a once a year affair but an every day prayer. We can start giving thanks for what is waiting for us in Heaven. Thank You Jesus for dying on the cross for our sins so that we can enter the gates of Heaven.

Have a Blessed Day! Follow Him! One Less Day to Go!

God blessed me today, when He:

_____
_____
_____

God used me today when I:

_____
_____
_____

I need to ask God to forgive me today for:

_____
_____
_____

_____

NOVEMBER 26

May the peace of our Lord Jesus Christ be with you!

> *"They were terrified and asked each other, "Who is this? Even the wind and the waves obey Him!"*
> Mark 4:41 NIV

Jesus had just calmed a storm by simply saying, "Quiet! Be still!" We know who He is today because of His word and the testimonies of the first Disciples. We serve The Almighty God. If the wind and the waves obey Him, why do we have such a hard time obeying? My brothers and sisters, may we learn to listen to our Lord and obey His word. May we learn to be quiet and still. One of the most difficult things for us to do is wait on our Father. May our faith be strong enough to trust Him and wait. So if you have been praying for something and God has not yet answered your prayer; have no fear; it is not that He is unable; it's just that He is not ready. Be strong in your faith and He will answer in His time.

Have a Blessed day! Follow Him! One Less Day to Go!

God blessed me today, when He:

_____

_____

_____

God used me today when I:

_____

_____

_____

I need to ask God to forgive me today for:

_____

_____

_____

_____

NOVEMBER 27

May the peace of our Lord Jesus Christ be with you!

> *"But may all who seek You rejoice and be glad in You; may those who love Your salvation always say, "The Lord be exalted!"*
> *Psalm 40:16 NIV*

May we seek to be like Jesus every day and not just during a season or special day. May we seek to obey Him every day. May we give thanks for His salvation every day. Let us be intentional about this. We will find what we look for. The Lord be exalted in our lives every day.

Have a Blessed Day! Follow Him! One Less day to Go!

God blessed me today, when He:

_____

_____

_____

God used me today when I:

_____

_____

_____

I need to ask God to forgive me today for:

_____

_____

_____

NOVEMBER 28

May the peace of our Lord Jesus Christ be with you!

> *"for, "Everyone who calls on the name of the Lord will be saved."'*
> *Romans 10:13 NIV*

There are many people, even Christians, who do not think that they need to be saved. The truth is we all need to be saved and the only way is through Jesus Christ. So may we call on His name every day. He will not get tired of hearing us call His name. Call His name first and last each day.

Have a Blessed Day! Follow Him! One Less Day to Go!

God blessed me today, when He:

_____

_____

_____

God used me today when I:

_____

_____

_____

I need to ask God to forgive me today for:

_____

_____

_____

NOVEMBER 29

May the peace of our Lord Jesus Christ be with you!

> *"I will not speak with you much longer, for the prince of this world is coming. He has no hold on me, but the world must learn that I love the Father and that I do exactly what My Father has commanded Me."*
> John 14:30 & 31 NIV

Jesus knew exactly what was going to happen before it happened. He knew that the devil will tempt Him in the garden of Gethsemane. He knew that He would not yield to the devil's temptations. Jesus showed His love for His Father and our Father by obeying 'exactly' what His father commanded. Do we do 'exactly' what our Father commands us to do? Do we even seek His guidance before taking action? May we learn to be like Jesus - resist the temptations of the devil and show our love for Him by doing 'exactly' as He commands - no compromise.

Have a Blessed Day! Follow Him! One Less Day to Go!

God blessed me today, when He:

_____
_____
_____

God used me today when I:

_____
_____
_____

I need to ask God to forgive me today for:

_____
_____
_____

NOVEMBER 30

May the peace of our Lord Jesus be with you!

> *"Be still before the Lord and wait patiently for Him; do not fret when men succeed in their ways, when they carry out their wicked schemes."*
> Psalm 37:7 NIV

Being still and waiting on the Lord can be one of the hardest things for us to do. But we must persevere and wait on the Lord. He sees all and knows all. We should not be envious of people who politic their way to worldly success. Our reward is in Heaven. Our father recognizes our efforts and will certainly reward us. Let us rejoice in saying - 'God made me what I am today!' and let us learn to be content.

Have a Blessed Day! Follow Him! One Less Day to Go!

God blessed me today, when He:

_____
_____
_____

God used me today when I:

_____
_____
_____

I need to ask God to forgive me today for:

_____
_____
_____

DECEMBER 1

May the peace of our Lord Jesus Christ be with you!

> *"God is our refuge and strength, an ever present help in trouble. Therefore we will not fear, though the earth give way and the mountains fall into the heart of the sea, though its waters roar and foam and the mountains quake with their surging."*
> *Psalm 46:1-3 NIV*

Commit the first line of verse 1 to memory - 'God is our refuge and strength, an ever present help in trouble.' Maybe you are not facing any trouble right now, maybe you are. The fact is we Christians will face a lot of trouble before we leave this earth. Jesus warned us that we will be prosecuted. Many believers are scared for their lives right now. We must know that 'God is our refuge and strength' in all things. May we always remember that He is with us and He is more powerful than anything or any one. Do not fear - trust in Jesus.

Have a Blessed Day! Follow Him! One Less Day to Go!

God blessed me today, when He:

_____

_____

_____

God used me today when I:

_____

_____

_____

I need to ask God to forgive me today for:

_____

_____

_____

DECEMBER 2

May the peace of our Lord Jesus Christ be with you!

> "But I will sing of your strength, in the morning I will sing of Your love; for You are my fortress, my refuge in times of trouble."
> Psalm 59:16 NIV

Experiencing trouble could be a blessing in disguise. We get to see God at work. When we are going through tough times we tend to call on Him more earnestly and depend on Him. So if you are going through some trials right now - praise the Lord! You will witness His majesty and be able to share how He carried and rescued you.

Have a Blessed Day! Follow Him! One Less Day to Go!

God blessed me today, when He:

_____
_____
_____

God used me today when I:

_____
_____
_____

I need to ask God to forgive me today for:

_____
_____
_____

DECEMBER 3

May the peace of our Lord Jesus Christ be with you!

> *"But now He has reconciled you by Christ's physical body through death to present you holy in His sight, without blemish and free from accusation—"*
> *Colossians 1:22 NIV*

This is what Easter is all about. Jesus sacrificed His physical body for you and me. Through His death and resurrection we are able to approach our Father as holy and without sin. This could be very challenging to accept, as the devil will have us believe that it is impossible. But we know that all things are possible with Jesus. So may we accept the forgiveness and the salvation that was made possible on that first Easter morning. There is no more need to beat up on ourselves. We are free!

Have a Blessed Day! Follow Him! One Less Day to Go!

God blessed me today, when He:

_____

_____

_____

God used me today when I:

_____

_____

_____

I need to ask God to forgive me today for:

_____

_____

_____

DECEMBER 4

May the peace of our Lord Jesus Christ be with you!

> *"They have lied about the Lord; they said, "He will do noth-ing! No harm will come to us; we will never see sword or famine.""*
> *Jeremiah 5:12 NIV*

It is very important that we have a personal connection with Jesus. He opened a way for us to come directly in His presence. He gave us His word. Let us seek His word and not become too dependent on others. When you hear or see people say or write about Jesus let us go to the word and validate what is being said. That way we will know the truth. The prophet Jeremiah warns us to beware of the liars and trust God so that 'no harm will come to us.'

Have a Blessed Day! Follow Him! One Less Day to Go!

God blessed me today, when He:

_____

_____

_____

God used me today when I:

_____

_____

_____

I need to ask God to forgive me today for:

_____

_____

_____

_____

DECEMBER 5

May the peace of our Lord Jesus Christ be with you!

> *"Come follow Me,' Jesus said, "and I will make you fishers of men." At once they left their nets and followed Him."*
> *Mark 1:17 & 18 NIV*

Jesus is still calling us to follow Him today. When we truly hear His call, we have no choice but to follow Him. He does not ask everyone to drop everything and literally follow Him. He simply wants most of us to follow His way today. Some are called to drop everything and follow Him. If that's your call, you will know. A believer will follow Jesus wherever he or she may be. May our lights shine so bright that many will want to follow Jesus also.

Have a Blessed Day! Follow Him! One Less Day to Go!

God blessed me today, when He:

_____

_____

_____

God used me today when I:

_____

_____

_____

I need to ask God to forgive me today for:

_____

_____

_____

DECEMBER 6

May the peace of our Lord Jesus Christ be with you!

"When they had seen Him, they spread the word concerning what had been told them about this child."
Luke 2:17 NIV

These shepherds have given us a good example to follow. First they went immediately to see what the Angel was talking about. They did not hesitate. Then, when they saw the baby Jesus and worshipped Him, they started sharing the good news with everyone they came in contact. Let us not get too caught up in the commercialization of Christmas and let us spread the good news of Christmas. Jesus is with us. It's not Happy Holidays - it's Merry and Holy Christmas!

Have a Blessed Day; Follow Him! One Less Day to Go!

God blessed me today, when He:

_____

_____

_____

God used me today when I:

_____

_____

_____

I need to ask God to forgive me today for:

_____

_____

_____

_____

DECEMBER 7

May the peace of our Lord Jesus Christ be with you!

> *"Philip found Nathaniel and told him, "We have found the one Moses wrote about in the Law, and about who the prophets also wrote -- Jesus of Nazareth, the son of Joseph."'*
> *John 1:44 NIV*

Who is your Nathaniel? Who do you need to share Jesus with? When we have found Jesus, we too must find a Nathaniel or several, and share Him with them. This is a great time to share Jesus with others, when they get so caught up in the decorations, parties and gift giving. We need to remind them why and what really started all this. We have found Jesus who was born on that first Christmas day.

Have a Blessed Day! Follow Him! One Less Day to Go!

God blessed me today, when He:

_____

_____

_____

God used me today when I:

_____

_____

_____

I need to ask God to forgive me today for:

_____

_____

_____

DECEMBER 8

May the peace of our Lord Jesus Christ be with you!

> *"But may all who seek You rejoice and be glad in You; may those who love Your salvation always say, "Let God be exalted!"'*
> *Psalm 70:4 NIV*

Seeking Jesus and desiring to be like Him is a joyful thing; not boring at all. So many people are looking for happiness in the wrong places or through the wrong medium; when all we have to do is seek Jesus and we will rejoice and be glad. I pray that God will be magnified in all of our lives. When people see us; when they interact with us - they will get a glimpse of Jesus.

Have a Blessed Day! Follow Him! One Less Day to Go!

God blessed me today, when He:

_____

_____

_____

God used me today when I:

_____

_____

_____

I need to ask God to forgive me today for:

_____

_____

_____

_____

DECEMBER 9

May the peace of our Lord Jesus Christ be with you!

> *"Yet to all who received Him, to those who believed in His name, He gave them the right to become children of God"*
> John 1:12 NIV

This Christmas season reminds us of the greatest gift that was ever given - Jesus Christ. Many celebrate the Christmas holidays but have not received THE GIFT of Christmas - Jesus. It is such an honor to receive Him. Then look at what comes with Him - 'power to become sons and daughters of God.' THE GIFT of Jesus is not a gift we put on a shelf or in a closet. It is a GIFT that fills us with power to deal with and overcome the evils of this world. We who believe and have received Him are sons and daughters of God. No harm can come to us. Amen and thank You Lord that You would find us worthy to be Your sons and daughters. Have you received THE GIFT of Christmas?

Have a Blessed Day! Follow Him! One Less Day to Go!

God blessed me today, when He:

_____

_____

_____

God used me today when I:

_____

_____

_____

I need to ask God to forgive me today for:

_____

_____

_____

_____

DECEMBER 10

May the peace of our Lord Jesus Christ be with you!

> *"He replied, "My mother and brothers are those who hear God's word and put it into practice.'"*
> *Luke 8:21 NIV*

Many hear God's word but do not apply it. Many go to church every Sunday and hear God's word but they do not obey. Jesus is very clear about those who hear His word and put it into practice - they are His family. Whose family are you a part of; Jesus or the devil? May we hear God's word and put it into practice every day of our lives on this earth. We are spiritual family.

Have a Blessed Day! Follow Him! One Less Day to Go!

God blessed me today, when He:

_____

_____

_____

God used me today when I:

_____

_____

_____

I need to ask God to forgive me today for:

_____

_____

_____

DECEMBER 11

May the peace of our Lord Jesus Christ be with you!

> *"We are hard pressed on every side, but not crushed; perplexed, but not in despair; persecuted, but not abandoned; struck down, but not destroyed."*
> *2 Corinthians 4:8 & 9 NIV*

This could be a very good reassuring verse for us believers in the light of what's happening every day. Many will be tempted to ask - 'Where was God? How can He allow this to happen to these innocent children?' These are all legitimate questions. The only one who can answer accurately is God Himself. It is at times like these we must be strong in our faith knowing and believing that God is still in control. He will reveal and explain everything when we join Him in Heaven. Meanwhile let us pray for the families and the communities - that the peace of God. that no one can explain will be with them.

Have a Blessed Day! Follow Him! One Less Day to Go!

God blessed me today, when He:

_____
_____
_____

God used me today when I:

_____
_____
_____

I need to ask God to forgive me today for:

_____
_____
_____

DECEMBER 12

May the peace of the Lord Jesus Christ be with you!

> "For what the law was powerless to do in that it was weak-
> ened by the sinful nature, God did by sending His own Son
> in the likeness of sinful man to be a sin offering. And so He
> condemned sin in sinful man, in order that the righteous re-
> quirements of the law might be fully met in us, who do not
> live according to the sinful nature but according to the Spirit."
> Romans 8:3 & 4 NIV

This is what the first Christmas is all about. We are powerless to save ourselves from sin. God is our judge - He cannot just ignore our sins. Someone had to suffer for our sins. Only Jesus was, and is qualified, being perfect - the sacrificial lamb. It is only when we become filled with the Spirit can we live according to the will of Jesus. So accept the real gift of Christmas - Jesus Christ and live in sin no more.

Have a Blessed Day! Follow Him! One Less Day to Go!

God blessed me today, when He:

_____
_____
_____

God used me today when I:

_____
_____
_____

I need to ask God to forgive me today for:

_____
_____
_____
_____

DECEMBER 13

May the peace of our Lord Jesus Christ be with you!

> *"He replied, "Whether He is a sinner or not, I don't know.*
> *One thing I do know, I was blind but now I see.'"*
> *John 9:25 NIV*

This man had a personal encounter with Jesus Christ. His main focus was what Jesus did for him. There are so many unanswered questions about our Lord. There is so much that's unknown to us. Then there is the known. The question we need to ask ourselves is 'What do we know about Jesus?' He is Lord. He became man and died for us because none of us could save ourselves. He is the only way to Heaven. So may we focus on the known and what's important. We celebrate Christmas because of the birth of Jesus.

Have a Blessed Day! Follow Him! One Less Day to Go!

God blessed me today, when He:

_____

_____

_____

God used me today when I:

_____

_____

_____

I need to ask God to forgive me today for:

_____

_____

_____

DECEMBER 14

May the peace of our Lord Jesus Christ be with you!

> *"I give them eternal life, and they shall never perish; no one can snatch them out of My hand."*
> *John 10:28 NIV*

Jesus came to give us eternal life. Let us receive this gift of eternal life. We may perish in this world but those who believe and have accepted the gift of eternal life know that death by any means is just a transition to Heaven and eternal life with Jesus. So we who believe and have accepted this gift, are not afraid of death. We are secured in His hands. Christmas is a time for receiving as well as giving. Receive the Gift of eternal life.

Have a Blessed Day! Follow Him! One Less Day to go!

God blessed me today, when He:

_____

_____

_____

God used me today when I:

_____

_____

_____

I need to ask God to forgive me today for:

_____

_____

_____

_____

DECEMBER 15

May the peace of our Lord Jesus Christ be with you!

"Peace I leave with you; My peace I give you. I do not give as the world gives. Do not let your hearts be troubled and do not be afraid."
John 14:27 NIV

The peace of our Lord Jesus Christ is the only real peace. Every other source of peace is temporary and comes with a price. The peace of Jesus Christ is unconditional. He does not ask for anything in return. When we have the peace of Jesus, we will not be anxious or doubtful and we will not be afraid. Receive the peace of Jesus Christ. That's another reason He came to leave His peace with us.

Have a Blessed Day! Follow Him! One Less Day to Go!

God blessed me today, when He:

_____

_____

_____

God used me today when I:

_____

_____

_____

I need to ask God to forgive me today for:

_____

_____

_____

DECEMBER 16

May the peace of our Lord Jesus Christ be with you! Merry Christmas to you and your family!

> *'But when the time had fully come, God sent His Son, born of a woman, born under the law, to redeem those under law, that we might receive full rights of sons.' (and daughters).*
> *Galatians 4:4 & 5 NIV*

God sent Jesus at the right time - His time. No one asked Him to come. He came because He wanted to come and redeem us from the law of sin. According to the law, we are all guilty. Jesus is the only one who could save us from the law. That's why He came on that first Christmas day. So as we celebrate and enjoy the material gifts and fellowship with family and friends; let us also receive the gift of redemption and 'full rights of sons and daughters.' Take some quiet time to thank Him for coming.

Have a Blessed day! Follow Him! One Less Day to Go!

God blessed me today, when He:

_____
_____
_____

God used me today when I:

_____
_____
_____

I need to ask God to forgive me today for:

_____
_____
_____
_____

DECEMBER 17

May the peace of our Lord Jesus Christ be with us!

> *"I issue a decree that in every part of my kingdom people must fear and reverence the God of Daniel."*
> *Daniel 6:26 NIV*

King Darius issued this decree after he witnessed Daniel in the lion's den and not being attacked by the hungry lions. We do not need a decree from a king who was scared to death. We have Jesus with us. We can choose to worship and reverence our God or not to. I pray that the Spirit of Christmas will remain with all of us every day for the rest of our lives here on earth; and we will sing songs to Him; go to church and share His love with others. That's worshipping God!

Have a Blessed Day! Follow Him! One Less Day to Go!

God blessed me today, when He:

_____
_____
_____

God used me today when I:

_____
_____
_____

I need to ask God to forgive me today for:

_____
_____
_____

_____

DECEMBER 18

May the peace of our Lord Jesus Christ be with you!

> "When Christ, who is your life, appears, then you also will appear with Him in glory."
> Colossians 3:4 NIV

Seven more days and we will celebrate Christmas the birthday or our Lord Jesus Christ. He came for us. He came to make a way for us to accept Him as Lord and Savior. Those who have really and truly accepted Him as Lord and Savior now live a life full of His Spirit. He is our life. We live for Him and to glorify Him. The old you and me is dead. The new you and me now live. When He comes again, we who believe in Him and live according to His will; 'will appear with Him in glory.' Is Jesus Christ your life; your whole life; not just a part of your life? Let us all make Him our whole life.

Have a Blessed Day! Follow Him! One Less Day to Go!

God blessed me today, when He:

_____

_____

_____

God used me today when I:

_____

_____

_____

I need to ask God to forgive me today for:

_____

_____

_____

_____

DECEMBER 19

May the peace of our Lord Jesus Christ be with you!

> *"Unless the Lord had given me help, I would soon have dwelt in the silence of death."*
> *Psalm 94:17 NIV*

We are all doomed without the help of the Lord! A life without the help of the Lord is headed for the depths of hell. May we learn to seek His help and guidance in all that we do - before we even start - not only when we find ourselves in serious trouble. Jesus came to make His Holy Spirit and power available to us. All we have to do is believe and accept. May you be filled with the power of the Holy Spirit that will help you overcome every temptation from the devil.

Have a Blessed Day! Follow Him! One Less Day to Go!

God blessed me today, when He:

_____

_____

_____

God used me today when I:

_____

_____

_____

I need to ask God to forgive me today for:

_____

_____

_____

_____

DECEMBER 20

'May the peace of our Lord Jesus Christ be with you!

"Come let us sing for joy to the Lord; let us shout aloud to the Rock of our salvation."
Psalm 95:1 NIV

As we come close to the end of another year, it could be a good thing to reflect on how our Lord has blessed us this past year. He has answered all our prayers. His answer may not have been what we expected at times; He may have even said 'no' sometimes. But we worship a God who always answers our prayers. So let us 'sing for joy' and count our blessings.

May you be able to recognize every blessing that the Lord will send your way; and may you embrace every opportunity to glorify Him in thought, word and action!

Have a Blessed Day! Follow Him! One Less Day to Go!

God blessed me today, when He:

_____

_____

_____

God used me today when I:

_____

_____

_____

I need to ask God to forgive me today for:

_____

_____

_____

_____

DECEMBER 21

May the peace of our Lord Jesus Christ be with you!

> *"But seek first His Kingdom and His righteousness, and all these things will be given to you as well."*
> Matthew 6:33 NIV

May we focus on seeking Jesus more. Place Him first in all things at all times. Our reward is 'all these things' - everything we need to live in this world. The reward should not be the main reason you seek Jesus. He knows what's in our hearts, so let us seek Him out of love and devotion. The blessings will come. We find what we look for. If we look for Jesus, we will find Him.

Have a Blessed Day! Follow Him! One Less Day to Go!

God blessed me today, when He:

_____

_____

_____

God used me today when I:

_____

_____

_____

I need to ask God to forgive me today for:

_____

_____

_____

DECEMBER 22

May the peace of our Lord Jesus Christ be with you!

> *"as far as the east is from the west, so far has He removed our transgression from us."*
> *Psalm 103:12 NIV*

This entire Psalm 103 is a great Psalm of praise, God's love for us and His greatness. When God forgives us, He really forgives us. He no longer sees our sins. So stop looking over your shoulder. Man may say they forgive you then remind you later of your wrongdoing. Not Jesus. He forgives and forgets. He sees the new you and me; the saved you and me; the redeemed and transformed you and me. He has washed us clean and separated us from our sins. Let us learn to forgive like Jesus. It is easy when you realize what He has done for you.

Have a Blessed Day! Follow Him! One Less Day to go!

God blessed me today, when He:

_____

_____

_____

God used me today when I:

_____

_____

_____

I need to ask God to forgive me today for:

_____

_____

_____

_____

DECEMBER 23

May the peace of our Lord Jesus Christ be with us!

> '"The time has come," He said, "The kingdom of God is near.
> Repent and believe the good news!"'
> Mark 1:15 NIV

Our Lord proclaimed this message over 2000 years ago. We must know that 'The kingdom of God is near' - nearer now than it was then. Every day, every breath, draws us closer to the kingdom of God. As we celebrate the birth of our Lord on that first Christmas day, may we remember why He came; and 'Repent and believe the good news' - a Savior is born.'

Have a Blessed Day! Follow Him! One Less Day to Go!

God blessed me today, when He:

_____

_____

_____

God used me today when I:

_____

_____

_____

I need to ask God to forgive me today for:

_____

_____

_____

DECEMBER 24

May the peace of our Lord Jesus Christ be with you!

> 'Today in the town of David a Savior has been born to you;
> He is Christ the Lord."
> Luke 2:11 NIV

Jesus did not come to receive gifts. He came to give Himself to us. The angel said 'a Savior has been born to you. I have spoken to many people who told me that they have not yet felt the spirit of Christmas. I myself have been a little low key about Christmas this year, then today the Lord showed me what Christmas is really all about. He placed a stranger in my way who was hungry and needed food. It was an honor for me to take her into the supermarket and buy her groceries. Then the spirit of Christmas hit me - it's not about receiving gifts - it's about giving. Try seeking out someone in need (a stranger) and give them something from Jesus. It's a blessing to be able to give.

Have a Blessed Day! Follow Him! One Less Day to Go!

God blessed me today, when He:

_____

_____

_____

God used me today when I:

_____

_____

_____

I need to ask God to forgive me today for:

_____

_____

_____

_____

DECEMBER 25

May the peace of our Lord Jesus Christ be with you!

"But You, O Lord, are exalted forever."
Psalm 92:8 NIV

In times like these we need to remember that the Lord is in control. May we look to Him and not be distracted by what's taking place in this world. These are times to seek His guidance and wisdom; to exalt Him; to make sure our light shines even brighter than before. We are children of the Almighty God. He will protect us from all evil. May we pray for one another and trust Him more. May we exalt Him every day; not just at Christmas and Easter.

Have a Blessed Day! Follow Him! One Less Day to Go!

God blessed me today, when He:

_____

_____

_____

God used me today when I:

_____

_____

_____

I need to ask God to forgive me today for:

_____

_____

_____

DECEMBER 26

May the peace of our Lord Jesus Christ be with you!

> *"For the Lord watches over the way of the righteous; but the way of the wicked will perish."*
> Psalm 1:6 NIV

How do we become righteous? How do we become Godly? The only way is through Jesus. We cannot achieve righteousness and Godliness on our own. We need the cleansing blood of Jesus Christ. When we accept Him as Lord and Savior - God knows if we are genuine or not -. (We cannot fool Him.); then we become righteous and Holy in His sight, because when the Lord looks at us, he does not see our sins. He sees Jesus. Be righteous and Holy.

Have a Blessed Day! Follow Him! One Less Day to Go!

God blessed me today, when He:

_____

_____

_____

God used me today when I:

_____

_____

_____

I need to ask God to forgive me today for:

_____

_____

_____

DECEMBER 27

May the peace of our Lord Jesus Christ be with you!

> *"Do not judge, and you will not be judged. Do not condemn, and you will not be condemned. Forgive, and you will be forgiven."*
> Luke 6: 37 NIV

If we are honest with ourselves we will admit that we judge and condemn every day. We find it hard to forgive. So when we are tempted to judge and condemn, remember this verse and know that we serve a God who does not condemn us, but saves us. When we find it hard to forgive, remember how much Jesus forgives us every day. When we compare everything with what Jesus has done and continues to do for us in spite of who we are, it is easier to not judge and easier to forgive.

Have a Blessed Day! Follow Him! One Less Day to Go!

God blessed me today, when He:

_____

_____

_____

God used me today when I:

_____

_____

_____

I need to ask God to forgive me today for:

_____

_____

_____

DECEMBER 28

May the peace of our Lord Jesus Christ be with you!

> *"Though the fig tree does not bud and there are no grapes on the vines, though the olive crop fails and the fields produce no food, though there are no sheep in the pen and no cattle in the stalls, yet I will rejoice in the Lord."*
> *Habakkuk 3:17 & 18 NIV*

What a statement of faith! Can we be as faithful today? What if the refrigerator was empty; there was no money in the bank; no phone to call someone for help, and you were all alone; can you and I say - 'Yet I will rejoice in the Lord, I will joy in the God of my salvation' - and mean it. Thank God we do not have to go this far to express our faith. May we not wait for drastic times, but may we rejoice in our Lord every day and thank Him for not testing us this way.

Have a Blessed Day! Follow Him! One Less Day to Go!

God blessed me today, when He:

_____

_____

_____

God used me today when I:

_____

_____

_____

I need to ask God to forgive me today for:

_____

_____

_____

_____

DECEMBER 29

May the peace of our Lord Jesus Christ be with you!

> *"Give thanks to the Lord, for He is good, His love endures forever."*
> *Psalm 107:1 NIV*

Our Lord is the only true 'good' being. His love is the only love that lasts forever. So let us give thanks, every opportunity we have, for He is good. Thank You Lord!

Have a Blessed Day! Follow Him! One Less Day to Go!

God blessed me today, when He:

_____

_____

_____

God used me today when I:

_____

_____

_____

I need to ask God to forgive me today for:

_____

_____

_____

DECEMBER 30

May the peace of our Lord Jesus Christ be with you!

> *"Why are you downcast, O my soul? Why so disturbed within me? Put your hope in God, for I will yet praise Him, my Savior and my God."*
> *Psalm 43:5 NIV*

There are so many reasons that can cause us to be downcast - the economy, politicians, fallen pastors, sickness, death, disappointment, etc. Believers are not immune to these situations. It's how we cope or react to these situations that make us different. When I was sick with a severe virus, I was tempted to be downcast - depressed. I hate being sick. But I remembered this verse. I suggest we all highlight this verse in our Bibles because we will be faced with situations that will tempt us to be downcast and disturbed. All of these situations are of the flesh, not of the Spirit. So when we are tempted to be downcast, may we quickly put our hope in God and Praise Him, our Savior and our God.

Have a Blessed Day! Follow Him! One Less Day to Go!

God blessed me today, when He:

_____

_____

_____

God used me today when I:

_____

_____

_____

I need to ask God to forgive me today for:

_____

_____

_____

_____

DECEMBER 31

May the peace of our Lord Jesus Christ be with you!

> *"Oh the depth of the riches of the wisdom and knowledge of God! How unsearchable His judgments, and His paths beyond tracing out!"*
> *Romans 11:33 NIV*

Many have tried to fully understand the power and wisdom of God. Some have even claimed to be more powerful. Some say He is a myth. But our minds are just too small to fully understand His wisdom and His way. That's where our faith comes to play. We believe what we have not seen and we hope for a place that's not of this earth. A day will come when we will know and understand everything. Meanwhile let us continue to be faithful.

Have a Blessed Day! Follow Him! One Less Day to Go!

God blessed me today, when He:

_____

_____

_____

God used me today when I:

_____

_____

_____

I need to ask God to forgive me today for:

_____

_____

_____

CPSIA information can be obtained
at www.ICGtesting.com
Printed in the USA
LVOW10s1039021116

511074LV00003B/4/P